Better Than Ever

7 SECRETS TO A *GREAT* MARRIAGE

by
David and Jan Stoop

Jordan
House

Meredith Books
1716 Locust Street
Des Moines, Iowa 50309-3023
meredithbooks.com

Printed in the United States of America
First Edition.
Library of Congress Control Number: 2007924915
ISBN 978-0-696-23623-5

Better Than Ever

Jordan House

Dedication

To all the couples who over the years have taught us
so much about great marriages.

Contents

Introduction

We have been married for more than 50 years and we've certainly had our times of struggle. So part of our learning about marriage comes from our own life experiences. Through the years we also have led marriage seminars and have met several thousand couples face-to-face at various stages of their marriages. So much of what we've learned has come from getting into the trenches with couples and helping them create the kind of marriages they have always wanted.

We are counselors who are pro-marriage. We love working with couples. We think of ourselves as marriage warriors—we fight for marriages! It feels like we are winning when we can help a couple restore their marriage.

We wish we could win every time. When we begin working with a couple, we sometimes think after listening to their story, *It shouldn't be too hard to help them get back on a good track.* But surprisingly some of the "easy" couples choose divorce. Then there are others who come, and we think, *Wow, this feels hopeless!* But it isn't, and they turn things around and restore their marriages, rebuilding them into beautiful, loving relationships. *What makes the difference?*

WINNING PRINCIPLES

We want to answer that question for you by sharing the secrets we have learned about what can make a bad marriage good and what can make a good marriage truly great.

You'll note as you read through the chapter titles that this isn't a guide on how to fight fair or how to communicate better—although you'll find help on these commonly written-about issues throughout this book. What we've tried to do is look at some of the deeper principles that aren't often talked about—those that can enrich any marriage. That's why we refer to them as *secrets*.

Our hope and prayer is that the secrets will get out! This book is designed to help you move your marriage in the right direction—to that place you dreamed about on your wedding day. Pressures facing couples today have evolved from when we married, but the winning principles remain the same. No matter the age of a couple or the stage of marriage, your relationship can improve. Your marriage can be better than ever.

MARRIAGE UNDER FIRE

Everyone seems to agree that marriage is under fire in the 21st century. The common perception is that a young couple getting married today has a 50 percent chance of getting divorced. To make matters worse, half of all divorces will occur within the first two to three years of a couple's marriage.

Religious beliefs seem to have no effect on these statistics because Christians are divorcing at the same rate as the general population. In some parts of the country, particularly in the Southern Bible Belt, Christians divorce at an even higher rate. In addition those who have already divorced and are now remarried are at even greater risk of divorce than those in their first marriages. And did you know that one-third of all newly married couples will have a physical altercation with each other within the first year of marriage?

REDEFINING THE INSTITUTION

Then there is the battle raging over how we are going to define marriage. Some states are rushing to pass laws defining marriage as a union only between a man and a woman, while other states are passing legislation that appears to give the go-ahead to same-sex marriage. Yet another controversial viewpoint comes from polygamist sects, such as groups in the West that have splintered from the Church of Jesus Christ of Latter-day Saints. The Christian church's voice appears to be weak in the debate over marriage; perhaps its silence comes from being accused of hypocrisy based on the high divorce rate within the Christian community.

In addition to marriage's modern struggles, the definition of family is being redefined as well. Our culture is seeking not only to normalize same-sex marriages but also to normalize cohabitation, fatherless homes, and single-parent families. Since 1960 the number of couples who are unmarried and living together has increased by more than 1,100 percent! That statistic only fuels the argument of the experts who are predicting the end of marriage as we know it.

QUESTIONS ABOUT THERAPY

And then there's the depressing news about marital therapy. Some studies say that marital therapy is successful only 20 percent of the time. If that's true, some say why bother?

A low success rate might exist because couples don't make the effort to get help until it's too late. Most couples wait at least six years from when a problem is first recognized before seeking help. By then their emotions are intense and frustration has built up to the point where one and maybe both partners feel like the marriage is hopeless.

GOOD NEWS ABOUT MARRIAGE

Pretty grim statistics. So why another book on marriage? Because marriage is a sacred institution ordained by God and it deserves our utmost attention.

Often we hear only about failures in marriage or how to fix the problems we encounter in marriage. We don't often hear about how marriages can succeed. Many Christians have joined the voices of our culture and have fallen prey to believing there is no hope for marriage. Bad news always grabs the headlines and provides fodder for countless talk show hosts to argue over whether something in our culture should die out or survive. Good news doesn't sell, or so they say, so the good news gets overshadowed. It's time we look at the good news about marriage.

Let's begin!

What's Good About Marriage?

CHAPTER ONE

There is good news about marriage. The positive side of the story is finally getting some attention. Researchers are working at identifying what makes a marriage successful. What are they discovering?

Well to start with, people still want to get married. In fact most of those who have gone through the pain of divorce want to marry again. And most of them do marry again. Did you know that 65 percent of high school girls and 58 percent of high school boys expect not only to marry, but to stay married to the same person for life? And that 83 percent of high school senior girls and 72 percent of high school senior boys say that having a good marriage is "extremely important"? And what about the fact that at any given time, 94 percent of married men say they are happier being married than being single? They say that being married has improved at least two important areas of their life—making money and having sex. In fact nearly three-fourths (73 percent) of married men say their sex life is better since getting married.[1]

The alarming statistic that shows the divorce rate in the United States to be 50 percent doesn't tell the whole story. It is really based on the fact that in any given region of the country during a given period of time there are typically twice as many marriages as there are divorces. The truth is that the divorce rate for first marriages is more like 39 percent, and the divorce rate for second and third marriages is closer to 60 or 70 percent.

When we lump all marriages together to come up with the 50 percent figure, we also miss some other interesting aspects of the marriage picture. Looking at marriage in the United States, the British news magazine *The Economist* pointed out that the percentage of divorces in first marriages based on education shows a lot of variation. "Among high school dropouts, the divorce rate rose from 38 percent for those who first married in 1976–79 to 46 percent for those who first married in 1990–94. Among those with a high school diploma but no college, it rose from 35 percent to 38 percent." In other words the better educated we are, the lower the divorce rate, even though it has been creeping higher in the 1990s compared to the '70s.

IT'S GOOD FOR YOU

There is also a large body of research that points out the benefits of marriage for both men and women, but especially for men.

Healthier, Happier Men

When men marry, their lives change dramatically. They become healthier and begin to lead more productive lives. "They work harder and do better financially than men who are not married. They are less likely to hang out in bars, to abuse alcohol and drugs, or to engage in illegal activities. They are more likely to spend time with relatives and to be involved in religious and community activities." [2] Much of marriage's positive effects on a man can be tied to his wife's influence.

Wives tend to provide men with a greater degree of awareness about their health issues, stabilize their husband's life routines, and when they work outside the home, add income that may take pressure off the man. But the interesting thing is that these benefits only apply to the married man. When you look at a man in an unmarried cohabiting relationship, these benefits are absent. His life is really no different from that of a single male. So marriage is more than just a woman caring about what's going on with "her man." The difference is typically attributed to a man's move to an altruistic lifestyle associated with the commitment made in his marriage. The single man can be self-absorbed and carefree, but the married man is expected to, and is more motivated to, take care of himself and the others in his life.

Another interesting change takes place in the man when he becomes a father. At the birth of his first child, a man usually settles down. His new role as a father apparently affects his physiology. Helen Fisher, a research professor of anthropology at Rutgers University, reports in a study that when men have high levels of testosterone, they also have high levels of divorce and low levels of commitment.[3] But if a man even holds any baby, his testosterone levels go down. And this is especially true when he holds his own first child.

For Richer, Not Poorer

Marriage also plays a powerful role in the attainment of wealth. How much better do married men do financially than single, divorced, or cohabiting males? Married men will earn an average of 40 percent to 60 percent more over their lifetimes.

In addition being happily married leads a man to look, on average, one-and-a-half years younger than his chronological age. A married woman will look one-half year younger. A divorced woman will look two years older than her chronological age, and a divorced man will look three years older than his chronological age. And at any point in time, a single, divorced, or cohabiting male is twice as likely to die than a married man.

It has been found that the better the marriage, the better each partner's health will be. In a happy marriage each partner will recover better when illness strikes. And if faced with a chronic disease, they will manage the disease better than their single or divorced counterparts. Unmarried women have mortality rates 50 percent higher than married women, and unmarried men have mortality rates 250 percent higher than married men. One way to understand this is to imagine two middle-age men from the same race, with equal incomes, and from comparable family backgrounds. At age 65 there is a 90 percent likelihood that the married man will still be alive, whereas there is only a 60 percent likelihood the unmarried man will still be alive!

One more statistic: In 2002, 64.6 percent of married men and 60.3 percent of married women said their marriage was "very happy." And over the years these percentages have been increasing slightly. Stable and satisfying marriages are crucial for the well-being of both men and women. They are even more important for the proper socialization and well-being of children. It was Cicero, in ancient Rome, who said, "The first bond of society is marriage."

Held in Honor

In God's society marriage is at the top of his list. God looked at the first human, Adam, and said, "It is not good for the man to be alone. I will make a helper who is just right for him" (Genesis 2:18). From Adam, God made

Eve. Then God presented her to Adam like a father presents his daughter to her husband-to-be at her wedding. And there in the Garden of Eden was the first wedding. Marriage was a part of the original creation. That's how important marriage is in God's eyes. And that's why the author of Hebrews urges, "Let marriage be held in honor by all" (Hebrews 13:4 NRSV). Obviously a healthy marriage is good for us![4]

THE "GOOD-ENOUGH" MARRIAGE

Having worked professionally with marriages for more than 30 years, we have found that bad marriages all tend to look alike. When a couple comes into Dave's office for help, we've found there's not much variety in what they bring to the table—the destructive patterns and problems are pretty much the same. These similarities have led to a rapid increase in the research that helps explain what behaviors and attitudes make a bad marriage bad. Consequently we can now identify what can make a bad marriage better and what can make a good marriage great.

But when one tries to define a "good" marriage, it's a different story. You will find a large variation in opinions on what a "good" marriage looks like.

We've all had the experience of spending time with another couple and marveling at the fact that, despite the negative reactions they have to each other, they stay together. They may argue a lot, one spouse may seem to be very quiet and uninvolved, or they may always seem to be in therapy of some kind—yet they stay together. Are these marriages good marriages? They don't seem to be bad marriages, but neither are they what we would call a great marriage. They have good components, but at best they are simply "good enough."

Child-Centered

For example we have observed marriages that have been very child-centered. Everything the couple talks about and just about everything they do is related to their kids. The wife is running one child here, while the husband is picking up another child to deliver somewhere else. Soccer, karate lessons, piano lessons, and ballet classes are just the beginning. There are also school activities and church activities the kids must attend. The only time the couple seems to interact is when coordinating who's running whom where and when. By the time the kids are in bed, the pair is too exhausted for any "couple time"—but they are committed to each other and enjoy the fact that all of their energy is devoted to their children. When the children are grown, the attention is then directed to the grandchildren. Their marriage lasts over the years, but there isn't much of a relationship between the husband and the wife. They might respond with something like, "Oh, we get along great..." and then turn the conversation back to talking about their careers or their ministries at church.

Career-Centered

Another type we've seen is the marriage that is career-centered. This is the couple that has postponed having children because they are both so caught up in their careers. And they are enjoying their successes—both for themselves individually and for each other. When they are together all they talk about is what is happening in their respective careers. Or one may be totally involved with a career and the other may be totally involved in community activities. Whatever they do is their sole focus. But when you ask them about their marriage, they really don't have much to say.

Who's in Charge?

We have seen marriages in which the woman runs everything and the man is rather submissive to the wife. Even though she "wears the pants in the family," they have worked out something that works for them. We've seen the opposite as well, where the man is clearly in charge and the woman takes the backseat in everything. In each of these cases, there is a clear hierarchy in the marriage, as opposed to a sense of equality between partners. They endure it over the years, but there is often an emptiness in the relationship because of the lack of interaction.

There are many other varieties of marriages out there: couples who fight a lot but love making up with each other; couples who seem to live separate lives, yet are clearly connected to each other; couples who seem to live from one counseling session to the next—the examples are as varied as the number of marriages observed.

We wouldn't call any of these marriages "good" but in each there are good parts. Research has found that when there are enough good things happening in a marriage, the marriage will survive, even in the presence of negative patterns and behaviors. But good parts aren't enough to make a mutually satisfying marriage. Most couples want something more.

More Than Parts

For years research has focused on what is wrong in marriages. The problems typically revolve around money, sex, in-laws, communication, conflict resolution, and anger issues. Therapists have tested different skill sets, looked at a variety of interventions, and compared theoretical approaches to marriage therapy looking for what would best fix whatever is wrong.

In more recent years through the pioneering research of John Gottman, a research psychologist at the University of Washington, and carried on by Scott Stanley and Harold Markman at the University of Denver, as well as by others, a large body of research has developed that helps explain what makes a marriage good, as well as what can predict marital success.

Judith Wallerstein, one of the experts on the effects of divorce on children, is among those who have defined the commonalitiesof what she calls "the good-enough marriage." For example, she points to the fact that in a good marriage, both husband and wife have "left their family of origin" to cleave to their partners.[5]

Leaving and Cleaving

This "leaving and cleaving" is a foundational issue in every marriage. Unlike in bad marriages, where many of the issues stem from the fact that one or both partners are still caught in a struggle of loyalties between their current spouse and their parents, those in good marriages have moved their loyalties to their spouse. It isn't an easy task, for leaving and cleaving puts both partners in somewhat of a bind. How do they leave without abandoning their parents and siblings whom they still love? In other words how can it be that leaving is not really leaving?

Finding this balance between leaving and cleaving is expressed in the struggle every couple faces in understanding what it means to become one as husband and wife. Good marriages have worked out the question of how one connects with his or her spouse emotionally and finds the oneness of marriage while at the same time remaining a separate self. It is a delicate balance between being drawn together and yet still being able to have one's own space and identity. In good marriages the couples have found this balance.

Problem-Solving Skills

Another common characteristic of a good marriage is that the couple has developed effective problem-solving skills. They are able to confront and effectively manage the inevitable crises that occur in every marriage. They have resolved, or are resolving, financial difficulties, problems with the in-laws, school problems with the kids, or even sexual difficulties. When faced with an obstacle, good marriages draw on some inner reserves to meet the crisis, as opposed to letting things get worse or even break up the marriage. In a good marriage, the couple perseveres and actually survives the crisis.

In good marriages the couples also know how to comfort and nurture each other. Instead of staying at the office late every day because he feels too much pressure at home or instead of pouring herself into the children so she can pretend the husband doesn't exist, a man and a woman in a good marriage have built together a safe zone within the home—a place where they can comfortably retreat from the pressures of life and the world.

Humor and Apologies

One other trait common to a good marriage is that there are those moments when humor and playfulness occur. These moments keep alive the images of early romantic times when the couple first experienced those feelings of love for each other. They may be fully involved in their careers or investing a lot of energy in their kids, but they have the occasional moment where their hearts connect over something funny or something nostalgic in their own relationship, and in that moment they reexperience those early feelings of love for each other.

In a brief talk on marriage, Rabbi Noah Weinberg boiled his advice down to three words: "Don't hold grudges."[6] Good advice. Someone else said that the three most important words in a good marriage are "I was wrong." Great advice! Having a really good marriage is what every couple desires. No one starts out his or her marriage with the hope that it will be just "good enough." Couples we see in counseling or meet at our workshops are there to improve their marriages and most of them want to go beyond having a good or simply a "good-enough" marriage to having a great marriage.

FROM GOOD ENOUGH TO GREAT

Talk to any couple about to get married and ask them, "So do you think you'll have a great marriage, or are you going to settle for just good-enough?" No, every couple starting out has the dream of a great marriage in their future. That is what Sal and Marie claim to have. They say they have a great marriage. So we asked them why they think they have moved their marriage beyond good enough to great. Marie answered first:

"I think one of the reasons we say our marriage is great is that we have never lost the feeling that we are first and foremost 'best friends' with each other. Our relationship started out as a friendship before it was romantic, and over the years we have worked hard at maintaining our friendship with each other."

Marie's comments hit on two things that describe a great marriage. First is the fact that they have worked hard at developing what they have with each other. A lot of good marriages just happen, but every great marriage is created by both spouses through hard work. They put energy into refining what they enjoy with each other. They have increased the positive things going on in their marriage.

The second point is that they have worked hard to keep alive the deep friendship they have with each other. They took what they started with and over the years nurtured their friendship—never taking it for granted.

Sal said, "What Marie says is very true, but what I think is equally important is that we have never shied away from conflict. The early years of our marriage were filled with conflict, and we weren't skilled at all in how to deal with those conflicts. But we hung in there with each other. Our commitment to being married never wavered, even when our emotions were running wild all over the place. But I think what we learned in dealing with conflict and frustrations provided the impetus for us to work harder and to grow stronger together."

Sal hit on an important point. Diane Sollee, founder and director of Smart Marriages, a national pro-marriage organization based in Washington, D.C., says that "the No. 1 predictor of divorce is the habitual avoidance of conflict."[7] She says that what many couples think is the high road—the absence of conflict—actually is the road that leads to a dead end. Couples believe that conflict will lead to divorce, so they avoid it. The opposite is true. Avoiding conflict inevitably leads to divorce! What can complicate the issue is the fact that when conflict is not managed, it escalates. This pattern is a high predictor of divorce, especially in the early years of a marriage. So we asked Sal why he thought their conflicts were not destructive to their marriage. He said:

"I'm not sure how to answer that. For us we've always looked back at those times and have given credit to the seriousness of our vows, especially that part that said, 'For better or for worse.' And those were often the worst times for us. But divorce was never an option to us. And I guess there was more than just a commitment—we really cared about each other. And when we were in a conflict situation, our caring for each other eventually would take over and soften what was going on. I can go back to what Marie said about friendship. Our friendship was always important to us. We both cared about each other and we communicated that to each other often. I think that gave each of us the sense that we were in this together and we were determined that we were going to stay in this together."

Attitude is everything. What we heard Sal say is that they worked hard at developing an attitude that didn't look for any escape clauses. But more importantly they went beyond simply staying together to developing an attitude that said they wanted their marriage to become the best it could possibly be. They worked hard to keep their friendship alive and strong. When inevitable troubles hit and they felt like they didn't like each other at the moment, they knew those feelings would pass and that their friendship and marriage would grow beyond the current issue.

"We have the basics. We've worked hard at communication, even though we've found out that we are very different in the way we speak and the way we listen. I'm very direct in what I say and speak with complete thoughts. Sal seldom completes a thought without jumping to some other subject. The problem we had to work on was not only how we talked, but also how we listened. I assumed Sal was speaking directly, and he wasn't. And he assumed I was only giving part of the story and he had the liberty to add in what he thought I was leaving out. That was a source of a lot of our early conflicts. Once we understood our different styles, we now laugh at the things that would have stirred up an argument."

For both of them, slowing down their interactions and focusing on really listening to each other was a breakthrough. This is extremely important. What couples typically do is react in conflict situations. But what they are reacting to is what they automatically think is going to be said or done. And they react to it before it even happens. Both partners do this and quickly they are off to the races, arguing and reacting to the same old things over and over. Slowing down the interaction stops our habitual reactions, and we often find that what is going on is different than what we first thought. Listening forces us to resist hasty reactions and understand each other more clearly.

Sal and Marie both said that learning to listen had helped them move on to a new level of enjoyment of each other in their relationship.

"I think one of the important things we experience today is a continually growing sense of oneness," Sal said. "The love we feel for each other now is more the result of our relationship. It regularly grows out of our involvement with each other. We have a common vision for our life together and of what we want from each other. And in addition we have the perception that each of us will do our part to achieve that vision."

Lots of couples spend a lifetime squaring off at each other. However, couples that experience a great marriage have moved beyond facing inward at each other to being able to stand side-by-side looking at a common vision of what they want in their marriage. They are purposely facing in the same direction—looking outward rather than inward.

Sal added:

"There's one more thing. I don't know if I can really describe it. We have been able to find meaning in the little things we do with each other. For example, we talk with each other on the phone several times a day. They are short calls, but those calls have a meaningfulness and specialness for each of us that is important. We have our shared jokes about things we've experienced over the years. And there are also the casual yet purposeful ways we touch each other—both when we are at home alone and when we are out with friends. We've found that these little things add up over time, and the positive feelings we have from these behaviors carry us through the tough times—which, by the way, we still have from time to time."

Carl Whitaker, an early family therapist and theorist, once said, "As much as I would miss my wife if she were to die, I would miss what we are together even more. Our 'we-ness,' our 'us-ness.' " We think this is what Sal was trying to say. Those reminders of their oneness built greatness into their marriage over time.

THE SECRETS OF GREAT MARRIAGES

In the chapters that follow, we want to go beyond what Sal and Marie have shared to describe what we have learned from more than 20,000 hours of counseling couples. They have taught us what we now believe are the seven secrets of great marriages.

Every couple begins marriage with a sense of what their hearts long for in the relationship. They want, as Ronald Reagan said, the "happiness of approaching the door at the end of the day knowing someone on the other side of that door is waiting for the sound of his or her footsteps." They want to be able to look at each other across a room and feel the spark inside that comes from knowing they are loved. They want to someday be that old couple who walk hand-in-hand with each other to the end of life's road. Who say to each other, as Robert Browning wrote, *"Grow old along with me. / The best is yet to be, / the last of life for which the first was made …"*

Each of the seven secrets will be discussed in a chapter, and then in the following chapter there will be exercises and questions you can discuss together as a couple to help you find practical ways to better apply the truth of that secret. Get ready to begin moving your marriage from good to great by focusing on what Jan and I have found to be the secrets of a great marriage. Welcome to the journey!

1 Summarized in Barbara Defoe Whitehead and David Popenoe, *The State of Our Unions: The Social Health of Marriage in America 2004* (Piscataway, NJ: Rutgers University, 2004).

2 Summaries of this evidence are in Linda J. Waite and Maggie Gallagher, *The Case for Marriage* (New York: Doubleday, 2000), and David Popenoe, *Life Without Father* (Cambridge, MA: Harvard University Press, 1999).

3 Helen Fisher, *Why We Love* (New York: Henry Holt, 2004).

4 All of these statistics are summarized in Whitehead and Popenoe, *The State of Our Unions.*

5 Judith Wallerstein and Sandra Blakeslee, *The Good Marriage: How and Why Love Lasts* (New York: Warner Books, 1995).

6 Found at www.aish.com/family/marriage/.

7 Published at www.smartmarriages.com/.

Making Friends With The "Enemy"

---

CHAPTER TWO

*"We'd have a great marriage
if only we could find
a way to resolve our problems."*

One of the major misconceptions we have of great or even good marriages is that they are problem-free. Well, if not problem-free, we at least think they are conflict-free.

Couples seem to believe this from the beginning of marriage. As I talk with young couples in premarital counseling sessions, many tell me of a common experience. They have a big blow-up, and then they struggle with the thought that maybe they shouldn't get married. They say something like, "We had a really big argument, and we still haven't resolved it. We don't know what to do. We're even wondering whether or not we're really compatible. Maybe we shouldn't even be getting married."

You can see the pained expressions on their faces as they reluctantly confess these feelings to me. What they are doing is believing the myth that when you are in love with each other, you will agree on everything. One of them might even ask, "After all don't people get divorced because they fight? If we don't agree on all the important things and have fights about them, how can we still really be in love with each other?"

Some couples skip the premarital counseling path, get married, and then are confronted with these feelings of incompatibility early in their marriage. After a few bad arguments, they become committed to the practice of avoiding any possible conflict situation or dispute by simply sidestepping any subject that might cause tension. Perhaps they did have some conflicts before they married; now when they have a major conflict, they become convinced they are failing in their marriage. Their fear of failure and fear of divorce keep them from talking about anything meaningful, and eventually they may even stop talking to each other altogether.

Their struggle seems to be compounded by the fact that most of their couple-friends don't appear to be having the same problems they are facing. Tim and Linda were convinced this was true. "None of our friends are having the problems we're struggling with," Linda complained. "Are we the only ones who can't get along?"

I, as their counselor, asked them if any of their friends knew they were having these painful arguments. "Well, no," Tim quickly responded. "We don't really want anyone to know. We haven't even told our parents— you're the only one who knows."

"Well if no one knows you're having this struggle," I answered, "what if these other couples are having some of the same issues you are having behind their closed doors? Maybe they are feeling the same way you're feeling about their arguments."

It's the rare couple who is willing to admit to their married friends that they are struggling in their marriage. Most suffer in silence as they wonder why they have so many quarrels. So the myth that marriages do better when conflict is absent continues to hold power over us.

THE TRUTH ABOUT CONFLICT

The truth is that it is healthy for couples to have conflicts, especially in the early days of their marriages. When two people begin to live together in marriage, there are a lot of adjustments both of them have to make.

We call the first 10 years of our own marriage The Great Tribulation. We struggled with all kinds of issues, and we didn't do a very good job of struggling. We look back at that time and know the only thing that kept us together was that we both believed there was no option of divorce— we were in this for the long haul. To get our marriage on a growth path took some growing up for both of us, and for Dave it also required some important mentoring. In that process we learned that the conflicts were what really pushed us forward.

But for some couples, the truth is hard to believe. Take Paul and Carol. They decided to see, as they said, "one more counselor before we sign the final papers for our divorce." Here's how our conversation went after they told me (Dave) that I was the "one more counselor" and we talked about their other experiences in marriage counseling.

Dave: "So what were some of the problems that led you to file for divorce?"

Paul: "Oh, we didn't have any problems."

Dave: "Well, what were some of the conflicts you experienced?"

Paul: "We've been married over 18 years and we've never had a serious argument of any kind—none that I can think of."

Dave: "You never argued about money or about sex or anything?"

Paul: "Never. We don't have any kids, and money was never a problem. We each did whatever we wanted. We traveled together a lot and that's something we'll miss—but, no, we never had even a squabble that I can remember."

Carol: "That's true. In fact our friends were totally shocked when they heard about our getting a divorce. They've all been convinced we have the perfect marriage. They still don't understand."

Dave: "Really?"

Carol: "All the other counselors were surprised as well. Especially when we told them that we had a relatively satisfying sex life together."

Dave: "So what made you decide to get a divorce?"

Paul: "I know this sounds trite, but over the years we had gradually grown apart. And about two years ago, we each came to the same conclusion at about the same time. For me it was like I woke up one morning and looked at Carol—and I don't mean this in a hurtful way— and thought to myself, 'If I had just met Carol, I don't believe I would even be interested in dating her.' I still love Carol, but for years now I haven't had that *in love* feeling about her. We really have each built our own lives separately to a point where the other person isn't really involved anymore. We have become strangers to each other."

I remember sitting there quietly for a bit, and then I asked, "Which one of you decided first to be absent emotionally in your relationship?"

I didn't really expect an answer.

Studies show that in marriages that are conflict-free, divorce is common around the 15- to 20-year mark.[1] These marriages are "emotionally dead." How sad that the conflict many couples work so hard to avoid in order to prevent divorce actually becomes a major cause of their divorcing!

Where there is no conflict, there is no passion. Without disagreements, over time the heart grows cold and distant, such as in Paul and Carol's marriage. Neither of them blamed the other for their own frozen heart. They knew that some time ago they each had shut down emotionally, withdrawn from the relationship, and pushed the other out.

The truth is that the absence of conflict in a marriage is often the most significant sign of a failing marriage. Author and counselor Gary Thomas says that "the absence of conflict demonstrates that either the relationship isn't that important to fight over or that both individuals are too insecure to risk disagreement."[2]

This certainly described Paul and Carol. As the couple and I explored the reasons why neither of them would risk disagreeing with the other, our discoveries clearly pointed to insecurities they both had developed growing up.

Both Paul and Carol had grown up in homes that were volatile and unpredictable. Both sets of parents screamed and yelled a lot. That was their normal conversational style. Paul's father and Carol's mother were also physically abusive. Paul often watched in horror as his father attacked his mother.

Both Paul and Carol had vowed at a young age to avoid, at any cost, the emotion of anger. They now admit that when they married, without ever discussing the impact of their family backgrounds on their own behavior, they again individually made silent vows not to repeat the patterns of their parents. And both of them took it to an unhealthy extreme. They completely avoided anything that might lead to a conflict or even to a misunderstanding, thinking that not fighting was a good thing.

I've never forgotten Paul and Carol. They ended up going through with their divorce. It was my first experience in talking with a couple who had what appeared to be the perfect marriage, but in reality they were living in emotional deadness with each other.

Dangerous to Your Marriage's Health

So the truth is, the avoidance of conflict is dangerous to the health of your marriage. One of the corollaries of avoiding conflict is that one or both spouses end up with deep hurts, which lead to silent resentments. In fact the interesting thing is that in failed marriages approximately two-thirds of the problems a couple faces will never be resolved in their lifetimes. That probably doesn't surprise you. But here is the surprise: In successful marriages approximately two-thirds of all problems a couple faces will never be resolved in their lifetimes. That's right: The statistics are the same for all couples.[3]

In failed marriages, when considering how a couple handles problems and conflict, one of two things happens. Either the couple begins to fight about the problems and those conflicts continue to escalate in intensity until their anger gets out of control, or the couple avoids the problems and they end up deadening their emotions. When couples escalate the hostility, the conflict intensifies quickly. Anger rules their marriage. Within a few short years—which may seem like an eternity to them—they are divorced.

Paul and Carol are an example of the second method of dealing with conflict. They avoided conflict completely, and it was just as fatal to the marriage, only with avoidance it just takes longer for the deadening process to kill the marriage. Either approach is fatal to the marriage.

So in marriages that succeed, as well as in great marriages, couples have somehow learned to get along with each other in spite of their problems. They have learned to do something different with their conflicts. The conflicts are there and are not avoided. It's what they do with the conflict that makes all the difference. Great marriages have just as many unresolved problems as do good marriages and failed marriages. But learning the seven secrets can make the difference between a good marriage and divorce.

SECRET NO. 1:

Make Friends With Your Problems

Couples in great marriages have learned that problems and conflicts are a natural part of a marriage. They know they can embrace their problems as a part of their growth process. They have made friends with their problems.

HOW GREAT MARRIAGES
MAKE FRIENDS WITH THEIR PROBLEMS

Let's talk with Sal and Marie again and ask how they learned to handle conflicts in their marriage.

Marie states:

"For one thing, we've learned to laugh at what used to drive us crazy. We told you about our communication problems—I'm very direct, and Sal is very indirect. It used to drive me crazy when Sal insisted that what I said wasn't what I had meant, for then he was sure his own interpretation of what I had said was more accurate. And he never says what he means. He is all over the place with his answers when I just want to say to him, 'Just say it—I can handle it.' What I can't stand are his uncertainties and backtracking. And I'm sure that my 'but you said' drove him equally crazy. But once we learned that our styles are different, we began to laugh in a fun way when I would say 'but you said.' And his response is always, 'but I meant.'"

Sal laughed as he added, "I had a hard time believing that Marie was really saying exactly what she meant. I mean I usually can't and I assumed she couldn't. So I was always trying to add meaning to what she said. Now when we get in those situations, one of us will comment on what we're doing and we usually end up laughing about it."

Of course Sal and Marie's ability to laugh at what used to make them angry or sad didn't just happen. It started with their desire to better understand their differences. That meant they had to discuss together what they felt was happening between them when they were talking. Perhaps the key was their ability to listen to each other and to let the other know they were listening.

What Listening Looks Like

Listening is a lost art in our culture today. We are programmed for sound bites. We love the magazine format with its short articles. Contemporary pressures have shortened our attention spans so that when it comes to listening, we all suffer from attention deficit disorder. As a culture we are becoming like the ancient Israelites whom God told Isaiah to tell, "Listen carefully, but do not understand. Watch closely, but learn nothing" (Isaiah 6:9 NLT). What was prophetic for Isaiah can be devastating for us in our marriages.

Listening is not an easy thing to do. It's hard work. If we are really going to listen, we have to temporarily forget about ourselves and our own needs and focus on the other person. Nothing bridges the separateness that divides us better than the experience of being listened to. The power of being heard can literally transform a relationship. To make friends with our problems in a marriage, we need to be better listeners.

Many couples simply take turns talking and call it communicating. But when they are finished, they don't really have the sense that they've been heard.

Sal talked about this: "I used to think I was really listening to Marie. I would get her so frustrated because I learned how to give back to her the exact words she had said. But then she would say, 'But you didn't really hear me!' and we'd be off on one of our major rows. I didn't know then that I needed to also listen to her heart and try to understand the emotions that were behind the words. That was hard for me, but persistence paid off."

We asked Marie how she got Sal to understand what she meant when she asked him to listen to her heart.

"I think what helped him the most was the word 'understand.' You can parrot someone's words but still not understand the meaning of those words. And I believe it is our emotions that give the meaning to our words. The tone of my voice, the look on my face—these are the kinds of things that give meaning to what I'm saying. And until Sal started to pay attention to these added pieces of information that went beyond the words, I didn't really feel like he understood me."

Good Questions Lead to Understanding

Genuine communication requires a sense of mutual understanding. One of the tools that Sal and Marie both worked at developing in their conversations was the role of questions. If we are going to move our marriage to greatness, we often need to slow down our communication process and ask pertinent questions. In the Bible, James tells us we need to be "quick to listen, slow to speak, and slow to get angry" (James 1:19). But when we do speak, sometimes a good question is the best thing we can say.

Good questions not only demonstrate to our spouses that we are trying to listen, but they also can clarify or define the issue being discussed. To better do this, as we formulate questions we need to ask ourselves, "*For whose benefit is this question?* Am I trying to make a point with a question, or am I really seeking to better understand what my spouse is trying to tell me?"

Marie shared how Sal struggled with this: "Sal had a way of asking the 'loaded questions.' They were designed to make a point. He would ask, 'How do you know ... ?' or 'Who says so?' or 'Why do you think that?' Or he would ask me a question that would have a simple 'yes' or 'no' answer and that would often end the conversation."

Sal added, "Once I started to get it that the goal was to understand and that it wasn't my job to fix the situation, I think I started asking better questions. And I think I really got it once I started asking Marie how she was feeling about what she was telling me. Now I can ask her something by simply putting an accent on a word that turns the sentence into a question."

Move From the State of Assumptions

One of the bad habits that keeps married couples stuck in unresolved problems is living in the state of assumptions. We can fall into the bad habit of wrongly assuming what the other person will say.

As counselors we often stop couples who are arguing about an issue and ask them to each take the other side of that issue. They start out looking a bit skeptical but soon are in a full-blown argument, only this time they are making the points their spouse was trying to make just a few minutes before. It was obvious that they each have the other's side memorized, yet they continue to go through the endless rhetoric, bickering about the same thing over and over. When they see how they have mimicked and memorized the other's discourse, they also see the futility of their arguments.

To move a marriage to greatness in the midst of problems that will not go away, we need to give up our assumptions and focus more on listening. (Or we need to learn how to short-circuit the process and even laugh our way out of the argument.)

Sal shared how they were able to do this. "For one thing Marie made a rule that we couldn't interrupt each other. I already noted that I have a tendency to read into what Marie is saying, so it was easy for me to figure out quickly what I thought she was going to say, and then I would interrupt her and argue against what I thought she was going to say. I wasn't always right. So we developed the 'no interruption' rule, and the 'no yes—but' rule. When we did that, I started listening better."

Breaking the Criticism/Defensiveness Cycle

Perhaps nothing blocks mutual understanding more than our natural tendency to become defensive. But to understand that, we need to see that this cycle always has two parts to it. First is what we always perceive to be criticism or an attack, followed by part two: our defensive behavior.

When your spouse says something that feels like criticism, you feel attacked. One of your defensive responses can be an effort to place the blame elsewhere: "It's not my fault!" Or you may act confused; our "I don't know" responses are often a defense against acknowledging what you've just said.

Withdrawal is a common defensive response of men. Many times when husbands respond by pulling away from their wives, they are simply trying to minimize the damage of the perceived criticism. Of course withdrawal never minimizes anything, as it is clearly experienced as a defensive posture.

Whining also can be a defensive response. After all it often worked when we were children. And then the hardest defensive response to identify is when we go along with what was said, but inwardly we are fueling our feelings of resentment and anger.

We're talking about the defensive *response,* but it always takes two to create the defensiveness, and it takes two to resolve defensiveness.

Here's what Sal and Marie did about this issue: "This was a biggie for me," Sal stated. "I was so quick to defend myself in our early years. I had grown up with a very critical mom, and so it was very easy for me to read my mom's criticism of me into Marie's 'helpful suggestions'. I would react so quickly, Marie didn't know what was happening."

Marie asserted:

"Boy, is that ever true. "I always thought I was just trying to be helpful, and I would get such a reaction from him that it would scare me. It seemed so out of proportion to me. When we were in counseling, you worked with Sal to separate me from his mom and then worked with me to better understand Sal's past. Then you worked with Sal in the sessions to slow down his reaction to me and to take himself out of the process and focus only on what I said. We would go over and over it in your office, and he gradually stopped defending. But I remember the first time Sal was able to not be defensive with me at home; we both broke down and cried when we realized that we were both changing the old patterns." (We will look at defensiveness in more depth in chapters 10 and 11.)

What Sal had to do was slow down his own mind. His mind was like a steel trap, ready to spring the minute he felt he was being attacked. It was like he had to loosen the spring so it wouldn't be so quick to react. "What helped me the most," Sal added, "was the effort to focus only on what Marie was saying to me. I worked hard at just responding to what she said, not to what it felt like."

Of course Marie was part of the process. She had to look for different ways of saying things to Sal. After she recognized how the way she said something would come across to Sal like his mother talking, she changed her approach to be softer and more open. The change helped Sal to not personalize things and react.

Our Attitude Is Foundational

We all need to adjust our attitudes to see that problems are not just problems—they are challenges that provide us with opportunities to grow as individuals and as couples. That's why the apostle Paul wisely wrote: "We can rejoice, too, when we run into problems and trials, for we know that they help us develop endurance. And endurance develops strength of character, and character strengthens our confident hope of salvation. And this hope will not lead to disappointment. For we know how dearly God loves us, because he has given us the Holy Spirit to fill our hearts with his love" (Romans 5:3–5).

Paul is talking about our attitude. He is not suggesting that we can rejoice that we have problems—we can rejoice *when* we have problems. The reason we rejoice is because of what the problems can produce in us, if we have the right attitude. Problems can produce endurance, and that endurance produces the important ingredient—strength of character. Couples in great marriages have used their problems to develop strength of character in each spouse. And that strength of character produces hope and fills us with love. What a promise!

CONCLUSION

So we've discovered our first secret—that partners in great marriages have learned that problems and conflicts are a natural part of a marriage and that they can embrace their problems as a part of their growth process. They have made friends with their problems.

Whenever a man and a woman move past the marriage ceremony and begin a life together, you have two individuals who are seeking to become one. Once they begin the work of building a life together, there are issues and conflicts that will always be a part of their relationship. And the ability to build a relationship with the ongoing issues, problems, and conflicts is basic to the development of a great marriage. Now let's look at some practical ways you can build this into your marriage.

1 John M. Gottman, *Marital Therapy: A Research-Based Approach* (Seattle: The Gottman Institute, Inc., 2000–2001), 42.

2 Gary Thomas, *Sacred Marriage* (Grand Rapids, MI: Zondervan, 2000), 162.

3 John M. Gottman, *Marital Therapy*, 15.

The Situation

CHAPTER THREE Seems Hopeless

But Not Fatal

What feels hopeless at times may be the starting point for greatness. If that sounds paradoxical, we've found over the years that a lot of what makes a marriage great is paradoxical. For example our experience as well as a lot of research suggests that about two-thirds of the problems a couple faces in marriage will never be resolved. That can sound hopeless until you understand that the percentage of unresolved problems is the same in bad marriages as it is in great marriages—all couples struggle with chronic unresolvable problems over the life of their marriages.

The good news is that whatever those unresolvable problems are, they do not determine greatness in a marriage. They are not fatal. We don't create a great marriage by just resolving more issues. The important thing to learn is that although couples in great marriages have just as many unresolvable problems as anyone else, they've learned how to talk together about the issues. Instead of a problem leading them into an escalating argument, they have found ways to talk about the issues without getting into an argument.

In this chapter we're going to look at some of the ways we can break any destructive communication cycles we may be experiencing.

EXERCISES IN GOOD COMMUNICATION

Perhaps you have seen the poster that says, "I know you think you heard what I said, but I don't think you realize that what you heard is not what I meant." We don't hear each other. Usually it's the man who can repeat verbatim what his wife has just said, but she sits there shaking her head and saying, "No, that may be what I said, but you haven't the foggiest idea about what I'm trying to tell you." And the husband responds in frustration, "How am I supposed to know what she means if she doesn't say it?"

Would you guess that misunderstandings are one of the greatest opportunities for growth and intimacy in marriage? Many have defined intimacy as "into-me-see." And in light of our need to learn to listen better, we might say that intimacy occurs when two things happen: Both spouses are willing to let "into me see" and are willing to look "into me."

Let's look at how you and your spouse are doing on this.

Exercise 1: What You've Resolved

As you begin to work on the principles laid out in this chapter, discuss together three or four problem areas in your marriage that you have been able to resolve over the years. As you do this, consider these questions:

1. What do you think made these problems resolvable?
2. What were some of the skills you used to deal with these problems?
3. How did you keep your emotions in check as you worked on these problems?
4. How important was quality listening in the resolution of these problems?

Exercise 2: Saying What You Mean

How well do you communicate? Sal and Marie described themselves as having different communication styles. Marie said she is a *literal communicator*—she typically says what she means and means what she says. She speaks in complete thoughts and puts a period at the end of what she says. Sal, on the other hand, is an *inferential communicator.* He says less than what he means and assumes his listener can fill in what's left out. He speaks with ellipses.

The problem is compounded by the fact that we each listen in the same way we talk. Marie listens and assumes that all those who are speaking to her are also literal communicators. So she takes Sal at his word and wants to hold him to exactly what he said. When Sal listens he assumes all those who are speaking to him are saying less than what they mean, just as he does. So he hears Marie and then adds his own meaning to what she said.

Take some time now and talk about how you and your spouse each communicate. Are you literal or inferential in the way you talk? Are you literal or inferential in the way you listen? How has this affected the way you communicate? Take the time to work at listening as you talk about this. Each spouse will probably better describe the other's communication style than his or her own. What's really important here is to understand how you are heard by your spouse.

Exercise 3: Who's Being Defensive Now?

Here's a short inventory that will help you begin to work on your listening skills. There are two sets of statements—one for the husband to answer about himself and one for the wife to answer about herself. Respond to each statement by putting a numerical value in the first space following the question. Leave the second space blank—it's for later. You may want to photocopy these pages so you can mark them up.

You will rate your responses on a scale of 1–5.

1 means "never"

2 means "sometimes"

3 means "usually"

4 means "often"

5 means "always"

Husband's Inventory	**My Evaluation**	**Spouse's Evaluation**

When my wife and I try to have a conversation,

	My Evaluation	Spouse's Evaluation
1. I jump to conclusions.	_____	_____
2. I get defensive.	_____	_____
3. I overreact.	_____	_____
4. I try to fix things.	_____	_____
5. I clam up.	_____	_____
6. I interrupt.	_____	_____
7. I'm concerned about "accuracy."	_____	_____
8. I look for whom to blame.	_____	_____
9. I correct what my spouse is saying.	_____	_____
10. I give advice.	_____	_____
11. I have an agenda.	_____	_____
12. I feel listened to.	_____	_____
13. I'm concerned about who's right.	_____	_____
14. I'm concerned about being wrong.	_____	_____
15. I get loud.	_____	_____

Rate your responses on a scale of 1–5.
1—never
2—sometimes
3—usually
4—often
5—always

Wife's Inventory	**My Evaluation**	**Spouse's Evaluation**

When my husband and I try to have a conversation,

1. I jump to conclusions. _____ _____

2. I get defensive. _____ _____

3. I overreact. _____ _____

4. I try to fix things. _____ _____

5. I clam up. _____ _____

6. I interrupt. _____ _____

7. I'm concerned about "accuracy." _____ _____

8. I look for whom to blame. _____ _____

9. I correct what my spouse is saying. _____ _____

10. I give advice. _____ _____

11. I have an agenda. _____ _____

12. I feel listened to. _____ _____

13. I'm concerned about who's right. _____ _____

14. I'm concerned about being wrong. _____ _____

15. I get loud. _____ _____

Rate your responses on a scale of 1–5.
1—never
2—sometimes
3—usually
4—often
5—always

After you have finished the evaluations, set aside enough time so you can talk together about your responses. Discuss your evaluation of statement No. 1 for yourself. Then ask your spouse how he or she would rate you on statement No. 1. Write that rating in the space to the right of yours. When your spouse's evaluation differs from yours, spend some time talking about the statement before moving on to the next question. Complete the inventory in this manner.

The Process of Communication

This exercise is designed to help you begin to work on being nondefensive as you talk together. Here are some principles that can help you be less defensive as you talk:

- Listen solely with the purpose of understanding what your spouse means.
- The person listening cannot judge, interrupt, or offer rebuttals. To really do this, you will need to silence your inner voice and focus on what your spouse is saying.
- As the listener, try feeding back to your spouse what he or she has just said. When your spouse agrees that you have "got it," then you can respond. And then it is the spouse's turn to listen and feed back to you what has been said.
- This is a way to talk about how you perceive your own listening habits and to listen to how your spouse experiences your listening habits. If you feel yourself being attacked or feel yourself becoming defensive, slow things down and comment on what you are

experiencing. You might say: "Does this feel like criticism to you?" Or: "I'm having a hard time listening right now; this feels like criticism, and I'm feeling a need to defend myself."

- When anxiety or tension is building in your conversation, try this: Stop talking about the subject of the conversation and talk instead about what you are experiencing inside. Talk about the process of your conversation rather than the subject of your conversation. In other words talk about what you are feeling at that time. Are you anxious? Are you getting angry? Are you feeling attacked? When you understand each other in terms of the process, you can return to the subject or set another time and place to continue the conversation.

JUMPING TO CONCLUSIONS

One of the benefits of slowing down our communication process is that we are also slowing down our inclination to make assumptions about what our spouse means or is going to say. Sometimes we do know what our spouse is going to say, but in those cases we aren't working on assumptions—we're basing our conclusions on previous conversations that have taken us down a familiar path.

What we mean by assumptions is the tendency to attach motivation to what our spouse is saying. Usually we make negative motives the root of our assumptions.

Exercise 4: Unmasking Your Assumptions

Take the time to slowly talk together as you finish the following sentences:

When we talk about _____,
    I typically assume you mean _____.

When you say _____,
    I typically assume you mean _____.

When you get that _____ look on your face,
    I usually assume you are feeling _____.

When I think back to one of our discussions about _____,
    I am sorry that I assumed you meant _____.

Now talk about some of the other assumptions you have made or felt your spouse has made in past discussions.

WHEN THE PROBLEM'S NOT THE PROBLEM

Often unresolvable problems seem so small that we feel we are being nitpicky, especially if we talk about these problems to a counselor or pastor. We've had couples describe to us the issues they are struggling with, and then they act almost embarrassed about what they just told us— "because the issues really seem so insignificant."

We tell them there are no insignificant problems. What feels minor is really something you feel safe disagreeing on, and it allows you to avoid facing the deeper issue behind the so-called "insignificant problems." It may provide cover for something simply too scary for you to identify, let alone discuss.

Great marriages, though, have gone beyond the insignificant issues to being able to dialogue about the deeper things that are underneath the presenting issues.

Exercise 5: Going Undercover

Let's look at what might be behind some of the so-called minor issues you and your spouse go 'round and 'round about. Think back over the past six months. Identify five issues you have had difficulty talking about together. Or list five of the things you always seem to argue about. Write them in the spaces below.

1. _____

2. _____

3. _____

4. _____

5. _____

Now comes the hard part. Take each of the issues you identified and talk about what it could represent. Look for the theme of the issue.

For example if one point of discussion revolves around money, you may uncover that what money usually represents at a deeper level in a marriage is power and control, or safety. So if money issues plague your arguments, talk instead about the balance of power in your marriage or look at the control issues—who feels controlled, who feels out of control, or how your handling or not handling money makes you feel safe—or not.

Sometimes the way we handle our money represents a different deeper issue. We've talked with couples who keep their money separate. They each have their own bank accounts. Their savings may be in a joint account, but not their spending money. For many of these couples, the separateness of the way they handle their money represents the lack of oneness in their marriage. They argue about the fairness of the way the bills are paid and what money belongs to whom. The idea of a common pot threatens the separateness they still hold onto in their relationship.

On another subject perhaps one of your recurring issues has to do with the in-laws or some intrusive relative. In this case look at loyalty issues. Issues involving sex are often related to anger and resentment that haven't been expressed or haven't been understood. Sometimes a generalized feeling of anger or resentment toward the spouse has to do with a goal or dream that has been frustrated or blocked.

You may have difficulty identifying what's behind some of the problems you face. But remember, you probably aren't going to resolve the issue. What you want is to be able to talk to each other and feel like you not only hear the other's words but hear the other's heart as well.

WHO IS RIGHT AND WHO IS WRONG

We love the look on a couple's faces when, after they have given us opposite descriptions of the problem that brought them into counseling, we say to them, "We want you to know that we believe both of you are right." They look at us as if we've lost touch with reality. The truth is, they are both right, though neither one is completely accurate. What they are describing are their subjective experiences of the problem they are facing.

Most couples come to counseling with the idea that if only their spouse would change, then their problems would be resolved and their life together would be great. So they are hoping that we, as counselors, will quickly arbitrate the issue and place the blame appropriately—which is on the other person.

What you miss when you get caught up in trying to fix blame is that nothing is being done to deal with the issue. And if your goal is to place blame, you are only fueling defensive behavior in the one you are trying to blame.

So here's the goal: Give up the need to place blame and work on dialogue. And as you do this, realize that in relationships all truth is subjectively experienced. So you are both right, but probably neither of you is totally accurate.

AN EXERCISE IN LISTENING

If you've had any problems talking and listening about the suggestions in this chapter, here is an exercise that will help each of you to listen. We call it a "dualogue" because it is a dual monologue.

Exercise 6: The Duologue

First, set aside 30 minutes at the same time each day for two weeks. Get a timer that can be set to 15-minute intervals. Flip a coin to decide who gets to talk for the first 15 minutes; it doesn't matter who begins. Each of you will also need to have a pad and pen to take notes of what your spouse says. The reason you must take notes is that you cannot respond that same day to anything your spouse says during the exercise—that's why it doesn't matter who talks first.

Next, pick a recent disagreement to talk about, and whoever goes first begins to present his or her side of the issue. As Spouse A talks, Spouse B takes notes about what is being said. This is important: Spouse B cannot interrupt, defend, or explain at all—until the next day. When the timer goes off, Spouse B takes the floor and makes his or her points about the same subject, being careful not to respond to anything Spouse A said in the first 15 minutes. The same rules apply to each. At the end of 30 minutes, you must put the timer away and stop talking about that issue until the next session. In fact you cannot talk about those issues at any other time except during the 30-minute duologue.

Now on the second day, it's Spouse B's turn to start. Here is when he or she can now respond to what Spouse A said the previous day. Spouse B can also make any new points he or she wants to make—all with Spouse A carefully taking notes about what is being said. Then at the 15-minute mark, Spouse A takes the floor and responds to Spouse B's monologue from the previous day. He or she also can add any points desired. You continue this each day for two weeks, always delaying your responses a day and carefully keeping notes of what you are being told.

We've seen couples who were constantly fighting begin to confine their arguments to the 30-minute duologue. They told us that taking notes forced them for the first time to really listen to their spouse. They also found that after a week or so they were inclined to reduce the 30 minutes to 20 and then to 10. What made the difference was not the resolution of the issues but the sense of each being heard by their spouse. When each spouse began to have the sense that they were being heard, they needed less and less time to "discuss" the problems.

TALKING IT OUT

If you've worked through the exercises in this chapter, you are in the process of mastering one of the major building blocks of a great marriage: good communication. Remember, you can no longer say, "We'd have a great marriage if only we could resolve all of these problems." Great marriages have issues and problems, but the difference is that the couple in a great marriage has learned how to really listen to each other's hearts as they talk together about the recurring issues.

Making friends with your unresolvable problems involves the following:

- Understanding the differences in the way you talk and listen and learning to laugh about them
- Knowing that defensiveness always follows criticism
- Doing away with assumptions
- Learning to recognize the problem behind the problem
- Understanding that placing blame never helps

No Fear

"We'd have a great marriage if only my husband weren't so afraid of real intimacy. He thinks that intimacy only means sex."

Relationships are hard work, and a marriage relationship is even harder work. Part of the reason for the added tension within a marriage relationship is that there are two opposite tasks involved in a healthy marriage relationship: oneness and separateness. We desire to become "one" with our spouse and come to marriage with that goal. Then the question arises as to which one we will become—you or me? And that is the second movement in a healthy relationship—the desire to still be me in the midst of our being we. How do we balance our oneness with each other's separateness?

Let's look at what typically happens in a marriage. During the honeymoon stage, the couple is striving for oneness. They only think about the "we." The "I" is incidental. We could diagram it like this:

You can see that at this stage there is a lot of the "we" and very little "I." The couple has a lot of togetherness but very little sense of self or autonomy. As the honeymoon wears off and the couple begins to settle in, conflicts start to develop. Neither wants to lose his or her sense of self, so each begins to protect his or her independence by moving away from each other. Soon the marriage can be diagrammed more like this:

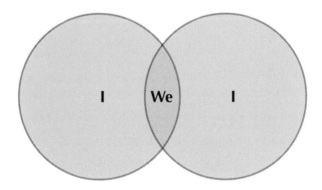

Now there is too much autonomy, and the desired closeness no longer exists. A couple may go back and forth between closeness and autonomy in an effort to find a balance. Their success in this dance of intimacy will depend in large part on how secure they are in their attachment styles.

A SECURE ATTACHMENT

How we work through the opposing movements required in a marriage relationship has its roots in our first relationships. We can illustrate this point through the birth of one of our grandchildren. When Jonathan was in the womb, he was in a perfect environment. All of his needs were met before he even experienced them. The womb was a quiet, safe world. Then came birth, and it was like Adam and Eve being expelled from the Garden of Eden. He left that perfect world to enter a very imperfect world.

We got to see Jonathan right after he was born. After a few minutes of admiring how wonderful he was, we watched as the nurse took him into the nursery and put him on a special table to clean him up. Well, first they turned on bright lights so they could really see him. Remember, he had been in darkness for nine months. Then they started to scrape him clean. I know they were very gentle, but nothing had ever touched his skin before. After he was clean, they stretched him so they could measure him, then they weighed him and took footprints. Finally they put some stuff in his eyes, wrapped him up, and put him in a bassinet where we could watch him fall asleep. What a welcome into this new world!

But the "welcome" wasn't finished. A few hours later, Jonathan woke up crying. He was experiencing his first need: hunger! And because he didn't know how to eat and his mother didn't know how to breastfeed him, a coach came to help with the process. Finally his hunger was satisfied and Jonathan fell back asleep.

We might say that Jonathan's first task in living in this strange new world was to find some way to make it feel safer. His relationship with Mom and Dad, as well as with the rest of the family, was designed to accomplish that task. That's why babies are so cute—it helps us fall in love with them. And our love and attention draws them close to us; that makes them feel that this new world is safe after all.

Thus we can say that the first movement in life is *toward* something. And the first important emotion is love. And if there is enough love, the baby begins to learn to trust those who love him or her.

Now around six to eight months, Jonathan began to work on his second primary task in life. No longer was he content just cuddling and being loved all the time. Now when we reached to hug him, he began to push us away. Soon he began to crawl and then to walk. And have you ever noticed that when children begin to crawl or walk, they are always moving away from us? (Have you ever seen a toddler chasing his mom? No, it is always the mom doing the chasing.)

This urge is not about us—it's all about wanting to explore this new world they are in. It's as if Jonathan were saying, "I've seen enough of you guys—I know you are there. I feel safe enough now to want to see more of the world." It is not fear at work here. One might say it is more of a natural curiosity we all are born with. It's a drive toward autonomy.

One way this has been described is to call the mother, and to some degree the father, a fortress of safety. An infant who feels safe begins to venture out of the fortress to explore the rest of the world. But when it gets scary, he or she comes scurrying back to the safety of the fortress. I remember this vividly illustrated with Jonathan when he was about two. We were at an outdoor mall with beautiful areas filled with flowers. He was happily exploring. When it came time to leave, his mom and dad called him, but he was engrossed in what he was doing and ignored them. Finally one of us said, "Hey, Jonathan, goodbye—we're leaving." He stopped short—took a second to think and then immediately turned and ran back to his "fortress."

This is the foundation of all of our relationships as adults. They are composed of two competing movements. One movement is the desire to move toward our partner, which is the movement of love. The other movement is the desire to move away, to develop—or retain—some degree of autonomy or separateness.

The ideal situation is when love is perfectly expressed, and the balancing movement of autonomy is perfectly permitted in a marriage. But none of us grew up in that perfect environment because none of us had perfect parents. And if our parents were perfect, that would have set in motion a whole different set of problems for us. Perfect togetherness would prevent parents from teaching us how to deal with conflict. God designed the world so that parents only have to be good enough, and the developing child is always ready to give grace when the parent messes things up—to a point.

THE INSECURE ATTACHMENT

Mom and Dad are the ones who create a safe fortress for their children. Children coming from a relatively normal environment that balances love with healthy limits on autonomy will grow into adults who are secure in their ability to build a healthy marriage relationship—to experience secure attachments. But a lot of us didn't grow up in that healthy environment. Our ability to feel secure in our adult relationships is marred. What happens when Mom and/or Dad didn't provide a safe fortress for us? What if the limits were too rigid or were unclear? What if the safe fortress was there some of the time but not consistently, or maybe wasn't there at all?

The outcome can be one of three faulty forms of relating: the avoidant attachment, the anxious attachment, or the fearful attachment.

The Avoidant Attachment

What happens when the safe fortress isn't safe or when it is unavailable? What happens when a parent dies or leaves during those early years? Or when the mother and father are emotionally unavailable, overwhelmed, or distant and cold? The result is that we grow into adults who have learned to be self-sufficient. When we learn at an early age not to trust anyone else and that we cannot depend on anyone else to take care of us, and when we continue these patterns as adults, we will become very reluctant to let anyone else—even a spouse—get close. The result for us in our marriages is that as much as we long for a close, intimate relationship with our spouses, we are uncomfortable with that closeness when we begin to experience it.

Closeness feels controlling, and control issues are big for those who experience the avoidant attachment. Closeness also demands too much emotionally. You may have problems even making a commitment to marriage because it is frightening for you to give up independence. Trust is also a major issue. When pressed you may trust little parts of yourself to selected people, but in the end you only really trust yourself. After all that's what you've had to do from the beginning—you learned early that you had only yourself to depend on. So your efforts at closeness are always overpowered by distancing (avoiding) behaviors.

The Anxious Attachment

What happens to us when the safe fortress is always under repair while we are growing up? We come running for shelter, only to find that one of the walls that provides safety is down. What is supposed to be safe doesn't feel safe. Perhaps Mom is sick a lot, so sometimes she is there, but other times she is unavailable. Or Mom and Dad are always fighting and talking of divorce. Children in these situations are often seeking reassurance that everything is going to be OK. They become clingy and need more than they can get.

The fear of abandonment is a major theme in their relationships. As an adult, when you have an anxious attachment style you often seek to become one with your spouse. If you could just be "joined at the hip" you believe you would feel secure; you won't be abandoned; your spouse will not leave. But at the same time, you struggle with feeling flawed deep down inside and feeling unworthy of being loved. So you need to keep the focus on your spouse's flaws through criticism in an attempt to keep your own flaws hidden.

The Fearful Attachment

The fearful attachment style is developed in a child who is afraid to run back to the supposedly safe fortress, for it has never really felt safe. At times it may have been safe, but those times are more than offset by the overall feeling of being unsafe. Verbal, emotional, or even physical abuse is part of the experience. The desire for closeness is there, but fear keeps the child away from what he or she desperately wants and needs. Children typically blame themselves for the lack of safety in their fortress, and they try harder to be perfect, thinking this will cause the significant adults to make things safe. But it is all to no avail. Inside the child feels unworthy of being loved, and fear is the basic response in his or her adult relationships. His or her basic fear is being abandoned.

Adults with a fearful attachment style often marry someone who is needier than they are, such as an addict, alcoholic, or irresponsible type of individual. And the result is no safety in adult relationships. As they did in childhood, they struggle to cover up abandonment issues, working harder and harder to try and make the relationship work.

THE ROLE OF FEAR

You can easily see how all relationships tend to put us in a quandary—especially the marriage relationship. Because one of the most basic desires every person has is to be loved unconditionally and because no one has ever grown up in the perfect environment, we all fear in some way what we want most: love. We end up in this quandary because love and fear are opposite emotions. The apostle John understood this when he wrote that "perfect love expels all fear" (1 John 4:18). We fear love because we are imperfect people who cannot love perfectly.

So think about how that hurts you in marriage. When you love someone, you want to move closer to the one you love. But when you are afraid of anything, you want to move away from what you fear. So your love draws you closer to your spouse, but your fear makes you want to run away. And when this occurs in marriage, we often become caught in what has been called the "pursuer-pursued" or "push-pull" marriage relationship.

One spouse is moving toward the other in love, while the other person is pulling away in fear. Finally the one moving toward the other in love gives up and begins to move away. The one being pursued senses the lack of being pursued and fears losing the other person, so the pursued becomes the pursuer. This back-and-forth movement can continue for years as our fears limit our ability to really love.

When you have had an insecure attachment history in your early years, you are more likely to encounter distress in marriage. You can see how the avoidant, the anxious, and the fearful styles of attachment work against the closeness we want in marriage. Whenever your spouse says or does something that reminds you of your early experiences, you withdraw, which only intensifies the precipitating behaviors that set in motion your withdrawal in the first place. All three forms of attachment—avoidant, anxious, and fearful—probably also play into the attachment issues of your spouse.

What is it you fear in loving relationships? There are a number of things that come to mind. You may feel fragile; therefore being wrong becomes threatening. You may fear rejection or ridicule. You may struggle with feelings of unworthiness and fear being found out. You may feel like you're an impostor and must keep that a secret. You may even fear that your secret thoughts might be read by the other person and then you will be seen as incompetent, cruel, judging, or having some other negative quality. Many of us fear being seen as a failure.

The list could go on and on and could be as varied as the number of people being interviewed on the subject. So let's go deeper. What are the basic fears we all struggle with to some extent in significant relationships, and especially in marriage? There are two deeper fear issues that we all face to some degree. They are: 1) the fear of being controlled by someone and 2) the fear of being abandoned by someone.

The Fear of Being Controlled

When our attachments are less than secure, one of the ways we compensate is to protect ourselves from being controlled by the other person. Individuals with the self-sufficient style of attachment struggle the most with this fear, although they would probably resist saying they are motivated by fear. "I just like being in control of my own destiny" they might say, or "I have a hard time with other people telling me what to do."

Sometimes this fear is more subtle and expresses itself through a spirit of independence. In a marriage that independence may come across as being responsible. It can be seen in the husband who is committed to his work, to service in his church, and to his kids' activities, but who has very little time left over for his marriage relationship. However, it's hard for him to recognize this as fear-based because he is being so responsible about all the things he's doing. But if he can see that he is using his responsible behaviors in a way that is creating an avoidance of his spouse, he may begin to see and acknowledge his fear of being controlled by his spouse.

Wives may struggle with this fear as well. She might pour herself into her work or into her friendships. Her independence may lead her to become overly involved with her children and their activities, thus limiting ways her husband can exercise control over her or her schedule. Again, these are responsible ways of behaving, but when the behaviors have an underlying purpose in maintaining a sense of independence that keeps her from feeling like she is being controlled, it is destructive to the marriage relationship.

The Fear of Being Abandoned

If you have an attachment style that is anxious or a style that is fearful, you typically will struggle more with the fear of being abandoned. You work hard at your marriage relationship. You act very responsibly about ensuring that the "we" in marriage is being nurtured, even if you are the only one nurturing it. Your efforts to keep your spouse involved in the marriage may only play into the fear of being controlled, but you can't let up in your efforts because that opens you to the reality of the abandonment fear.

When you struggle with the fear of abandonment, you may become needy and even clingy at times, while at other times you may be standoffish in an attempt to protect yourself from even the possibility of abandonment. You may even go so far as to sabotage a relationship and make the other person leave. Then you can think you weren't really abandoned—the other person left because of what you did, not because of who you are. You may think, I can handle me driving away my spouse better than I can handle him or her just leaving me.

THE PUSH-PULL OF TWO FEARS

Of course these two fears—being controlled and being abandoned—don't operate in isolation. You will experience both of them, though one will be predominant in your experience, in your behavior, and in your marriage.

For example fear of abandonment may cause you to try very hard in your marriage. But when you find that you are closer to your spouse than you are comfortable with and you start to feel controlled or smothered, you back off from him or her in an effort to regain some comfortable personal space. But then your fear of abandonment rises up again and you start to move back toward the other person, setting in motion a repeat of the pattern just described. When you add into this equation the particular fears of your spouse, you can see why true intimacy takes a lot of work and requires a foundation of trust.

As noted earlier what we see in a distressed marriage is that the couple eventually establishes a marriage that is ruled by these fears. Their relationship may be based on so many surface fears that they aren't even aware of the deeper fear issues of control and abandonment. They tend to either continue to argue over what they think they are afraid of, or they shut down and act as if the surface fears no longer exist.

In a good-enough marriage we see a different pattern. Most of the superficial fears have been faced and may still be there, but they don't dominate the marriage relationship. The couple, however, still has not faced the two basic fears; they have settled into a pattern that accommodates these two fears rather than facing them and working out their relationship. Here's how their marriage might be diagrammed:

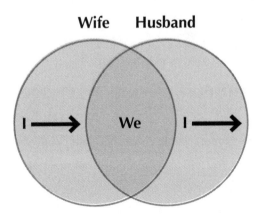

In this illustration the wife's primary fear of abandonment causes her to expend most of her energy on the togetherness, the "we." She is very responsible in terms of the marriage but does little for herself. Her life is one of willing sacrifice for the marriage and the family. She doesn't realize that she is on this giving treadmill because underneath it all resides her fear of being abandoned, and she doesn't consciously want to face that fear.

The husband puts most of his energy outside the marriage. He may be a responsible person, so his energy goes to good things like work, his kid's soccer team, teaching Sunday School, and other good activities for a husband and father. He doesn't realize that he pours his energy outside the relationship because that numbs the fear of being controlled or consumed, which he might experience if he put more energy into the marriage.

A lot of good marriages represent the push-pull of these competing fears. One fear dominates in one person and the other fear dominates in the other person. But those who are in great marriages have broken free from this cycle. They have and may still be working through their fears of closeness and intimacy, but they are not locked into a pattern that keeps them stuck in the pursuer-pursued roles. They are able to move freely in the relationship, no longer being ruled by their fears.

SECRET NO. 2:

Face Your Fears

Couples who experience great marriages have had the courage to face their basic fears rather than allowing the fears to control their relationship. In addition they are willing to look at the roots of those fears and are able to talk together about what they are learning and experiencing. As a result they are able to experience a deeper level of intimacy.

As you can see in the drawing, both husband and wife have a healthy balance in that they are both responsible for the marriage relationship—the "we"—and both have retained enough of a sense of the self—the "I"—that the fears of abandonment and control are kept out of the picture most of the time.

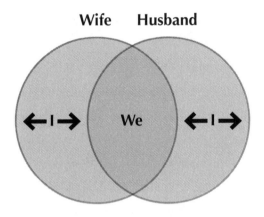

THE THREE CANDLES

It's interesting at a wedding to watch what the couple will do with the unity candle—the large one between the two smaller individual candles that represent the bride and groom. One wedding involved a very symbolic act in which the mother of the bride and the mother of the groom went up to the altar at the beginning and lit the two candles that would be used by their son or daughter. Did the couple keep their individual candles lit or blow them out, as is common?

When they left their individual candles lit, we almost wanted to stand and cheer. It is possible they didn't fully understand that they were laying the groundwork for a great marriage. This is a very important truth for any newly married couple to grasp. There is the "we" of the marriage, and there are still the two individual "I's" within the marriage.

The tradition of blowing out the individual candles is to emphasize the "oneness" of marriage, so if you blew out your individual candles after you lit the unity candle, take no offense. This is just something that is symbolically important to us as counselors, and so we refer to it here to illustrate the point.

Genuine intimacy is built as you face your fear of either being abandoned or being controlled. Intimacy is developed through being comfortable with who you are as you seek to become one with your spouse. Intimacy involves two whole people coming together to create a new "us," as opposed to two incomplete people trying to complete themselves through the other person. When you face your fears directly, those fears lose their power to intimidate you.

CONCLUSION

Couples tend to either lose their own identites in a marriage, or they continue to feel put upon and fight against the feeling of being controlled by their spouse. Many of their unresolved issues will revolve around these two basic fears—the fear of being either abandoned or controlled. It's not an easy task to keep the balance between the "we" and the "I." Those who have worked at finding and keeping this balance will, with one voice, say: "The effort was worth it. We wouldn't trade what we have learned in the process for anything!" They are the couples experiencing great marriages.

In the next chapter, we'll look at some ways you can build a better balance between the "we" and the "I" in your marriage.

There's Nothing To Fear But Fear Itself

A simple definition of the kind of intimacy we are talking about is this: the joyful union that comes when two people learn together both how to give love and how to accept love.

The path to this joyful union starts out easy enough. Think back to when you first met your spouse and how easy it was to talk about anything for as long as you wanted. It was easier then because there was so much to learn about the other person and you knew so little. Fear hadn't raised its ugly head yet either. If we look at those early years, what we were experiencing was actually a feeling of closeness, not intimacy.

CLOSENESS VERSUS INTIMACY

It is important that we differentiate between closeness and intimacy. There are a number of things that can make us feel close to our spouse. A satisfying sexual experience, a mutual crisis, grief, an exhilarating experience—any of these or similar experiences can make us feel close for a period of time. But that is not intimacy. Intimacy involves a "being known" that is mutual. It involves not only learning more about the other person but the other person also knowing more about yourself and letting the other person know more about you as well.

What do you believe about the subject of intimacy? What were you taught? Often our faulty beliefs keep us from the intimacy we desire. Take a moment to assess your beliefs about intimacy. Read each of the following statements and decide which you believe are true and which are false.

Exercise 1: An Intimacy Checklist

	True	False
1. If my spouse really loves me, he or she will always know what I want or need to be happy.	_____	_____
2. The best indicator of a good marriage is a good sex life.	_____	_____
3. If we are really close, we should be able to point out each other's errors and shortcomings without feeling threatened.	_____	_____
4. My spouse either loves me or doesn't; if not, there is nothing I can do to make it any different.	_____	_____
5. The more we can disclose—both good and bad information—to each other, the more intimate we will become.	_____	_____
6. Keeping the feelings of romantic love alive is necessary to fuel an intimate relationship.	_____	_____
7. I have to feel love toward my spouse before I can help us grow more intimate.	_____	_____

How did you answer? Did you answer true to any of the statements? If you answered false to every statement, your beliefs about intimacy are accurate. Each of the statements is a myth. Let's look at them one by one.

Myth No. 1: Intimacy Is Being Able to Read Each Other's Mind

The desire to have your spouse read your mind is really an extension of a childhood wish, and it seems an innocent enough goal to have in a marriage. As adults we often long to be taken care of automatically. We think, "The person I love will know what I need and provide it for me even before I know I need it."

This idea finds some reinforcement in the early stages of a relationship. You often experience those moments of "mind reading" that feel so wonderful. During the early stages of a relationship, we are more attentive to each other, so we can quickly recognize what's needed or desired at a given point in time. Later in our marriage relationship, we tend to take for granted the needs of our spouse, and we need to be reminded or told what's in our spouse's mind.

One of the more common expressions of this myth we often hear is the statement "It isn't the same if I have to ask for it." Or "If I have to tell you what I need or want, then somehow something is lacking in our marriage." We always ask the person who voices this objection, "Isn't your goal to experience intimacy? If it is, then why not ask for what you want?" The reality is that no one, especially your spouse, can really know what you need or want in most situations unless you tell him or her.

Myth No. 2: Sex Is Intimacy, and Intimacy Is Sex

Physical intimacy and emotional intimacy are two different things. You can have sex without emotional intimacy, just as you can have emotional intimacy without sex. Yet many people see the two as the same. In fact we sometimes substitute sex for emotional intimacy without knowing the difference.

Many times we hold on to this myth because we are afraid of affection. Affection makes us feel vulnerable, and when we feel vulnerable, we encounter our fear of abandonment or being controlled again. Or one spouse may be afraid of affection because it is always a precursor to sex. "I only want to experience the closeness of affection and not have sex, because I don't know how to set this limit," is a common sentiment. In addition the husband or wife who holds on to this myth often wants to have sex after an argument in order to feel okay about the marriage. They reassure themselves about the marriage by having sex together.

Myth No. 3: People Who Love Each Other Can Accept Constructive Criticism

Believing this myth is similar to believing the lie that "Sticks and stones will break my bones, but names will never hurt me." Many of us were taught that rhyme as a child. We'd shout it at the bully. It didn't help then, and it doesn't help today because names and words can really wound us deeply.

Often as we were growing up, we learned to minimize criticism from a parent in order to hold on to the idea that the parent loved us. If we were to validate our experience of harshness and criticism, we would have difficulty believing that we were worthy of their love. Logic and rationality were meaningless to us as children, and they are just as meaningless to us today as adults when we feel criticized and unloved.

In fact criticism is one of the love-killing and marriage-killing behaviors that has been recognized in research. There is no such thing in a marriage as "constructive criticism." Criticism always sets up a defensive response, which never fosters intimacy and love. This is because criticism is usually an attempt to "fix" a spouse.

Myth No. 4: Someone Either Loves Me or Not—and That's That!

This is a common thought today, that someone either loves me or they don't love me. It's black and white; there's no middle ground. So, according to this, if the feelings of love go away, then love is gone for good. A spouse who has this experience may say, "I still love him (or her), but I'm not *in love* anymore."

Our standard response to either of these statements is, "That's not really an issue. Rather we want to know when you stopped *acting in loving ways* to each other?" Usually the response is that it has been some time since any loving behaviors have happened. No wonder the feelings of love have vanished.

The feelings of love usually wither and dry up in a sterile, arid environment. The lack of loving behaviors leads to the deadening of the feelings of love. Love needs to be nurtured and fed. The way couples in great marriages feed the feelings of love is through the behaviors of love. Giving a back rub; bringing home flowers for no reason; calling your spouse from the office during the middle of the day; reaching over and holding their hand—these are some of the behaviors of love. The apostle Paul gives us a description of some behaviors of love when he writes, "Love is patient and kind. Love is not jealous or boastful or proud or rude. It does not demand its own way. It is not irritable, and it keeps no record of being wronged" (I Corinthians 13:4-5). When we see love as the consequence of the behaviors of love, we can better understand that when the feelings of love have dissipated, they can be restored through the behaviors of love.

Myth No. 5: Knowing Everything About the Other Person Is an Essential Part of Intimacy

Honesty is a basic ingredient of intimacy. But we sometimes confuse honesty with knowing everything possible about our spouses and revealing everything about ourselves. It is a myth that intimacy results from "telling everything" or being totally open. Your spouse may not be able to handle some of what you disclose. Or sometimes total disclosure of yourself destroys the mystery of personhood that is so important to an intimate relationship.

Intimacy is not based on how much you know about your spouse; it is built on how much you are able to satisfy your *mutual* needs. These mutual needs represent the desire for more in the relationship. Often these needs grow out of unmet childhood needs that have been brought into a marriage. You need to understand that having those needs and other current needs met in both the husband and the wife is the foundation of an intimate marriage, not how much you know about your spouse.

It's hard to know where to draw the line on full disclosure. The most important guideline you should use is to ask yourself, "Why do I want to know or share this information? and What is the primary motivation?" Check to see if you are motivated toward some wrong principle of openness that you mistakenly think will lead toward fully knowing each other. Do you find yourself saying, "We're going to be 100 percent honest in this relationship no matter what," as a need to clear your own conscience at the other's expense? Yes, we are to speak the truth—we'll look more at this in chapter 10—but it should always be tempered by love. (As the apostle Paul states in Ephesians 4:15, "Speak the truth in love.") The ultimate test should be to ask yourself, "Will sharing this information build a greater sense of intimacy?" You may be surprised at how often the answer is "no."

Myth No. 6: Romantic Love Is Essential for Intimacy
Many people realize this is a myth, but they are still governed by it. Many of the books we read and the TV programs and movies we watch reinforce this

myth. Yet today the expectation that romantic love can and should sustain an intimate relationship puts an incredible strain on marriages in our culture.

Romantic love has been described as sweaty palms, heart palpitations, obsessive thinking about the other person, and the belief that this relationship will meet all of our dreams. Think about the meaning of statements like "falling head over heels in love" and "I was swept off my feet." These are wonderful feelings designed by God to bring people together, but no one can maintain these feelings over the years.

The issue here is the concept of romantic love. We aren't talking about romance and doing romantic things with each other. Loving interaction, as we'll see in the next chapter, is an important ingredient in the building of closeness. Romantic love can be dated at least as far back as the Song of Solomon in the Bible. But our acceptance of it as an ideal goes back to the end of the twelfth century. Eleanor of Aquitaine and her daughter, the Countess Marie of Champagne, summoned her personal chaplain, Andreas Capellanus, to their palace at Poitiers and instructed him to prepare a manual on courtly love. Many of their husbands were off fighting in the Crusades, so they asked for help in defining how women would relate to the men who were left behind. Even though no one really reads the book—*The Art of Courtly Love*—anymore, its ideas still influence the way men and women relate to each other.

One of Capellanus' statements gives a taste of the problem he created: "We declare and we hold as firmly established that love cannot exert its powers between two people who are married to each other. For lovers give to each other freely, under no compulsion of necessity, but married people are in duty bound to give in to each other's desires and deny themselves to each other in nothing."[1]

Capellanus' work was not written to describe marriage relationships. It was written to describe "courtly" love—the illicit relationships between people in the promiscuous court of Aquitaine. Besides defining romantic love, he also laid the foundation for the idealization of women, the importance of gentlemanly courtesy, and the emphasis on the potent emotions felt in the beginning of a relationship. The part of his work to which we no longer give credibility is the "agony of a love that is unfulfilled." He taught that for love to be "true" love it could never be consummated— the couple could never fully act out their love with each other.

The writings of Keats, Dante, and Shakespeare; the operas of Wagner; television programs like *Friends* and *Sex in the City;* and movies like *Gone with the Wind* and *Love Story* have all shown the impact of Andreas' work. The truth is that in the long run, intimacy is related to romance, but has very little to do with romantic love.

Myth No. 7: Your Relationship Can Grow Only When You Feel Good About Each Other

Your relationship will grow only when you learn to work through those times when you really don't feel like doing the things that will make marriage work. A popular song said, "Loving you is easy 'cause you're beautiful." But there was no verse on what to do when *loving you is difficult because right now you look ugly to me* or *I feel ugly*. But that is precisely the time when couples in great marriages have gone to work on their marriage relationships. As we'll see in the next chapter, an integral part of a great marriage is the commitment we have to working on our relationship. That commitment keeps us living out the behaviors of love even when we don't feel like it. And the amazing thing is that when we do this, the feelings of love can and will return.

These myths about intimacy all work as barriers to the intimacy we really long for. As you've worked through these myths, it may be very clear to you that they are myths. But they still can seem attractive. It is important to recognize the hold any of these myths may be subtly asserting over your marriage relationship.

Talk with your spouse about your thoughts concerning each myth, identifying where you still see them at work in our culture today and where they may still be influencing your own attitudes and behaviors.

THE FACETS OF INTIMACY

People often say that men define intimacy as *s-e-x,* and women define intimacy as *t-a-l-k.* There is a lot of truth to this, based on our experience with couples. But it represents a very limited understanding of intimacy. Intimacy goes way beyond talk and sex.

In fact we have identified eight areas where couples with great marriages are able to experience intimacy with each other. They are: physical, emotional, conflict, creative, play, intellectual, work, and spiritual. First we'll describe each area of intimacy. Then you should evaluate how you are doing as a couple in each type of intimacy described.

1. Physical Intimacy
We'll start where husbands typically begin when it comes to a discussion on intimacy. Physical intimacy is more than sexual intimacy in that it includes any mutually acceptable form of sensual expression. It involves affection, touch, and physical closeness. It is also more than sexual in that it is "the experience of sharing and self-abandonment in the merging of two persons, expressed by the biblical phrase to become one flesh."[2] Men typically begin with the physical and then move from there to the other areas of intimacy.

2. Emotional Intimacy

This is where wives typically want to begin, and their desire to start with this area puts it in its proper place because emotional intimacy is the foundation for all of the other facets of intimacy. Emotional intimacy is the knowing of each other's innermost selves. We are connecting on the level of who *we are* rather than on what we are doing. Talking together about the feelings and emotions related to events, actions, and experiences is the path to emotional intimacy. But emotional intimacy goes even deeper when we can share the effects that these events, actions, and experiences have on us.

3. Conflict Intimacy

This area is more difficult to develop because it involves staying connected to each other in the midst of a conflict. It is not just the ability to make up after a conflict, although that is part of it. Couples with great marriages are able to disagree, even strongly disagree, without the fear of being cut off by their spouses. The disagreement may escalate into a full-blown argument, but never at the expense of the connection. Because the connection stays intact, these conflicts aren't followed by long periods of pouting and silence. Because the connection with each other is never broken during the argument, both parties have other ways, such as humor, to end the argument. One of the ways couples maintain the connection in the midst of conflict is by touch. A hand on the other's forearm can completely change the tone of an argument because there is a connection.

4. Creative Intimacy

Creative intimacy involves things like creating beauty in and around the home or in bringing each spouse's different skills together to build something. It can also include the idea of working together for each other's growth. This facet of intimacy may begin with the creative act of bringing a child into the world. Nothing in a marriage is more creative than the birth of a child. How a couple responds to the birth of a child, especially the birth of the first child, or the adoption of a child, sets the pace for other forms of creativity in the marriage. Creative intimacy can also involve how a couple works together in parenting. In fact anything that calls on us together to use our imaginations leads to creative intimacy.

5. Play Intimacy

In the Bible's most famous chapter on love (1 Corinthians 13), the apostle Paul writes, "When I grew up, I put away childish things" (v. 11). It would be easy to interpret those words to mean that adults are to stop playing. This is especially true if you had a difficult time during your early childhood years. But notice that Paul does not say we are to put away "child-like" things; he points to "childish things." The healthy adult still knows how to play, and in a great marriage, the couple still knows how to have fun together. Playing together as a couple gives us energy and restores our sanity. This is an often neglected but extremely important facet of intimacy.

6. Intellectual Intimacy

Remember those stimulating conversations you had in the early stages of your dating? They were often quite literally mind-stretching. In great marriages couples continue to stretch each other's minds with stimulating conversations. They talk about more than just the weather or what to have for dinner. They share ideas from their reading, they discuss current issues, they attend lectures and plays and discuss their impressions of what they just experienced. They may even take a class together. There is a mutual respect for each other's minds and intellectual abilities.

7. Work Intimacy

Here's where the sense of partnership enters into the marriage relationship. This is the intimacy we experience when we are working together on anything from cleaning the garage to raising a family. Work intimacy requires discipline and motivation to make things even better. It is the intimacy we experience as we work together toward common goals, and it includes the good feelings we share when we reach those goals. It's the shared joy of a job well done that was accomplished together.

8. Spiritual Intimacy

This is an often neglected but very powerful facet of intimacy. It goes beyond just having a shared faith, attending church, or doing spiritual things together as a family. It is based on shared spiritual activities within the marriage, such as praying together as a couple,[3] reading the Bible to each other, or doing some other spiritual discipline together just as a couple. Studies have shown that when couples practice the discipline of praying together, they in effect divorce proof their marriage. Couples in great marriages have found behavioral ways to do spiritual things together as a couple. It's a natural part of their marriage relationship.

Exercise 2: Intimacy Inventory

Now that we have defined each type of intimacy, take some time as a couple to identify how well you believe you are doing in each area.

We'll use a scale of 0 to 7, with zero representing a total lack of intimacy in that area, and seven representing total fulfillment in that area of intimacy. The numbers indicate how you evaluate how well you as a couple are doing in each type of intimacy. It is your *subjective evaluation*. There's a chart for the wife and one for the husband.

Wife's Intimacy Inventory:

1. Physical Intimacy   0__ 1__ 2__ 3__ 4__ 5__ 6__ 7__

2. Emotional Intimacy   0__ 1__ 2__ 3__ 4__ 5__ 6__ 7__

3. Conflict Intimacy   0__ 1__ 2__ 3__ 4__ 5__ 6__ 7__

4. Creative Intimacy   0__ 1__ 2__ 3__ 4__ 5__ 6__ 7__

5. Playful Intimacy   0__ 1__ 2__ 3__ 4__ 5__ 6__ 7__

6. Intellectual Intimacy   0__ 1__ 2__ 3__ 4__ 5__ 6__ 7__

7. Work Intimacy   0__ 1__ 2__ 3__ 4__ 5__ 6__ 7__

8. Spiritual Intimacy   0__ 1__ 2__ 3__ 4__ 5__ 6__ 7__

Husband's Intimacy Inventory:

1. Physical Intimacy   0__ 1__ 2__ 3__ 4__ 5__ 6__ 7__

2. Emotional Intimacy   0__ 1__ 2__ 3__ 4__ 5__ 6__ 7__

3. Conflict Intimacy   0__ 1__ 2__ 3__ 4__ 5__ 6__ 7__

4. Creative Intimacy   0__ 1__ 2__ 3__ 4__ 5__ 6__ 7__

5. Playful Intimacy   0__ 1__ 2__ 3__ 4__ 5__ 6__ 7__

6. Intellectual Intimacy   0__ 1__ 2__ 3__ 4__ 5__ 6__ 7__

7. Work Intimacy   0__ 1__ 2__ 3__ 4__ 5__ 6__ 7__

8. Spiritual Intimacy   0__ 1__ 2__ 3__ 4__ 5__ 6__ 7__

THE WHEEL OF INTIMACY

Take the results of your inventory and create a wheel of intimacy for your marriage. The wheel consists of a spoke for each category of intimacy. Using one colored pen for the wife's responses and a different color for the husband's, estimate where your results would fall on each spoke (0 at the center; 7 at the tip). Here's an example:

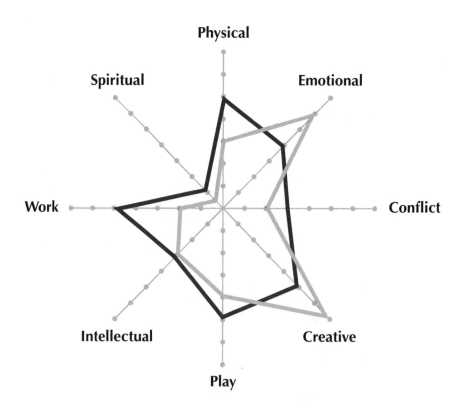

You see in this example that neither the husband's nor the wife's wheel is very round. The husband's responses are in red, and the wife's responses are in pink. In our example conflict intimacy and spiritual intimacy are both weak in comparison to the other types of intimacy. The husband and wife are in agreement in this area of intellectual intimacy. For them to find the balance for a great marriage, they can now identify the areas of intimacy that need work.

Now take the time here to enter the scores of each of your responses and see how your wheel looks.

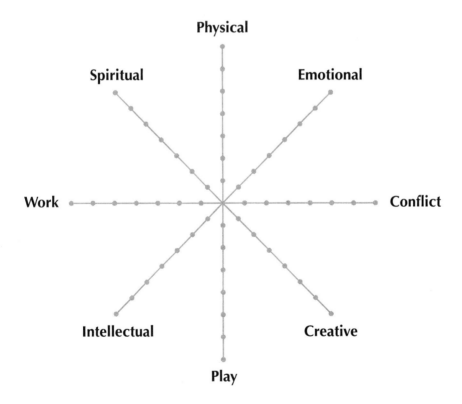

How does your wheel look? Any flat spots that need work? In a great marriage, the wheel will be rounder, showing a balance between each type of intimacy. Take the time now to discuss together how your wheel of intimacy turned out. Explore each other's needs as revealed in the weaker areas. Which of those needs are connected to unmet childhood needs? Discuss also what you can do together to get your wheel more balanced.

FACING OUR FEARS

As you discuss the facets of intimacy, especially in those areas where you've rated yourself on the low end of the scale, include in your discussion what you believe to be the roots of your avoidance of these areas of intimacy. Are you fearful of abandonment—that your spouse might leave you either physically or emotionally? Are you fearful of being controlled by your spouse if you open yourself in this area of intimacy? Are you afraid of failure? As you risk discussing your responses to these questions, you will be taking significant steps in the direction of achieving deeper intimacy together.

Here are some important rules to keep in mind during your discussion:

- Remember, it is not a question of being right. Deeper intimacy comes when we give up the need to be right.

- Focus on listening and asking questions when you don't understand what your spouse is saying.

- Stay connected during your conversation. Sometimes putting your hand on your spouse's forearm as you speak gives a symbolic sense of wanting to stay connected.

1 Andreas Capellanus, *The Art of Courtly Love* (New York: Columbia University Press, 1990)

2 Howard J. and Charlotte H. Clinebell, *The Intimate Marriage* (New York: Harper and Row, 1970), 29.

3 For more details on the practice and the benefits of spiritual intimacy, see our book David and Jan Stoop, *When Couples Pray Together* (Ventura, CA: Regal Books, 1995).

Know Love

CHAPTER SIX

"We'd have a great marriage if only we
could recapture the passion we used to
feel—if we could be 'in love' again."

"Love is one of the most intense and desirable of human emotions. People may lie, cheat, steal, and even kill in its name—and wish to die when they lose it. Love can overwhelm anyone at any age."[1]

These are the words of prominent Yale University psychologist Robert Sternberg concerning what he calls the "mystery of love." Some people who have tried to study love end up saying it is just a glob of intense emotional experiences that cannot be understood. Others have tried to break it down into so many pieces that they end up explaining nothing. Sternberg's research provides us with a very workable model of love, one that we will cover later in this chapter.

One of Sternberg's most important insights is that while love may draw a couple together, it is not what keeps a couple together. What is far more important to a couple staying together in a satisfying marriage is this: that husband and wife really like each other.

What's the difference between liking and loving? Perhaps one way to show the difference is to look at a couple who aren't married but who are at very different places in their relationship. Let's say the man is thinking about a future with this woman, getting married, and having children with her. He is forming a passionate loving attachment to the woman. He is experiencing love.

But the woman is merely enjoying the company of this man. She considers him a close friend. She looks forward to their times together, has fun with him when they are together. She misses him when they are apart, but she doesn't feel any strong attraction to him as a sexual partner. She just enjoys being with him and doing things together. She isn't even thinking about the possibility of marriage and children with this man.

They are obviously on different pages, and at some point the man is going to be deeply hurt in this relationship. He *loves* her while she *likes* him.

Research has shown that in great marriages the spouses really do like each other, and at the same time, they really do love each other. A strong marriage combines all the feelings of the man and woman in our previous example. Liking each other is the foundation for feeling close to each other and for feeling a sense of connection to each other, whereas love goes beyond the sense of connection to the "why" of our connectedness. In truth, in marriage both form the foundation of a truly loving relationship.

WHAT IS LOVE?

So what is love? We've used several good definitions of love over the years. One says that love is an emotional-volitional response to an intellectual evaluation of another person.

I (Dave) used this definition while teaching a college Sunday School class years ago, and after the class a young man came up to me and said, "I like that definition. I've been dating several girls, and I think it's time I get married. So I'm going to make that intellectual evaluation of them and decide who I'm going to marry!"

I wasn't sure I wanted to have that definition taken so seriously so quickly. The next week he introduced me to Linda as his future bride. Later I asked him how he had decided. He said he had made a list of all the positive things he liked about each of the girls he was dating. Then he wrote out what he thought might be the problems they would face as a couple. Then, after letting what he had written sit for a while, he went back to it to see what his emotional response was to his evaluation lists. Linda was the clear winner according to his heart's response.

Another definition says that love exists when the emotional and physical well-being of the other person are more important than your own.

How different those ideas are from some of our culture's common definitions. A famous (or infamous, depending on how you view it) line from the 1970 hit movie *Love Story* says, "Love means never having to say you're sorry." Or we hear the common statement about someone falling in love and never stop to think that if one can fall into love, one might fall out of love. Both actions are obviously unpreventable—we just can't control the emotion of love. We already examined some of these ideas when we looked at the myths about intimacy in chapter 4.

C. S. Lewis described love this way: "Love, in the Christian sense, does not mean an emotion. It is a state not of the feelings but of the will; that state of the will which we have naturally about ourselves, and must learn to have about other people."[2] This Christian contribution to the understanding of love is not only recognized by Sternberg but is incorporated into his definition. His research on love led him to develop a three-part definition of love. He defined love as consisting of: (1) intimacy; (2) passion; and (3) commitment. He called it the "triangle of love." Let's look at each of these components of love.

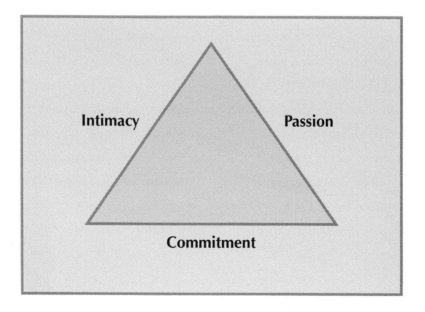

1. Intimacy

Intimacy, as a part of the definition of love, can be described as the feelings we have that make us feel close to a spouse, that make us feel connected and bonded to each other. Intimacy includes liking each other. One definition of love states that it exists when the welfare of the other person is as important or sometimes even more important than our own. This part of intimacy occurs when we think highly of our partners. We don't hold back ourselves, our time, our energy, or even our possessions. We are able to give support and receive support from each other. And obviously, to do this, we have to communicate with each other.

You can see that when these qualities are present in a marriage, we begin to trust our spouses more and more over time with more and more of ourselves. We gradually break down the walls that separate us. Intimacy is the foundation of love. It develops slowly and unevenly and is something we are always developing. We never fully arrive at intimacy with our spouses—we are always moving toward intimacy.

The building blocks of intimacy include being emotionally available and responsive to our spouses. In marriage we will experience intimacy with our spouses when we know they are there for us and that they are responsive to us. This can't be a hit-or-miss process—it must be there on a daily basis.

In addition to being accessible and responsive is the feeling of being accepted. Opposites do attract, though not necessarily total opposites. Where you are different from your spouse, you can become uncomfortable and seek to reshape him or her into your own image. But intimacy is built on the knowledge that we know what our differences are and accept the other as is. And as that experience of being accepted grows over time, we are able to reveal more and more of ourselves, causing intimacy to grow. Accessibility, responsiveness, and acceptance are ways that we are known to each other.

Another way of thinking about intimacy is that when each spouse knows that he or she is present in the other spouse's mind, even when they are not together, they are in an intimate relationship. Sal, in describing the intimacy in his marriage, said about Marie, "When I'm away from Marie, it's not like she stops existing in my mind. She is as real to me when we are apart as when we are together. It's like she lives inside of me and I take her with me everywhere I go. And I think I'm that way for her."

2. Passion

When we think of passion, we almost automatically think of the physical and sexual aspects of marriage. This is a powerful part of love. King Solomon described passion at its most ardent level in this way: "For love is as strong as death, / its jealousy as enduring as the grave. / Love flashes like fire, / the brightest kind of flame" (Song of Solomon 8:6).

The physical and sexual attraction we feel, especially at the beginning of a relationship, can be this kind of passion. But passion goes beyond just the physical. It involves the excitement we have at just being together, the sense of well-being we have doing just about anything together.

Michael Sytsma, cofounder of the Institute for Sexual Wholeness with his wife, Karen, points out that the experience of passion at the early stages of a relationship is the result of a powerful chemical present in our bodies that is stimulated when the other person is present. But that chemical "begins to fade and is replaced by a comfort chemical as our relationship becomes more committed."[3] The Sytsmas go on to point out that doesn't mean we must give up on passion in marriage. In many ways passion in marriage is experienced over time as caring for and about our spouses.

What stirs a sense of passion in a marriage over time? It can be described as a deepening of the thoughtful consideration shown in a marriage relationship. Also, as you peel away layers, allowing your spouse to see more and more of you and care more and more for you, you keep passion alive. One of the ways you can do this is to realize that the personality of your spouse is so complex it can never be fully known—you are always learning and growing. For example do you ever wonder what the color blue looks like to your spouse? Is it the same as you experience it? What is it about the music your spouse enjoys that makes it enjoyable? What does a steak taste like to him or her? These are just a few examples of the endless questions you can have about the way your spouse experiences life. These questions can keep the mystery of personhood alive in a relationship. How exciting it can be to realize that over the years we can still never fully know the other person; it is an ongoing adventure.

3. Commitment

It's interesting that the first two components of love involve both decision and emotion. Intimacy takes place when we first decide to spend time opening up to our spouses, and the feelings of intimacy follow. Passion begins as an emotion, but then it is kept alive by making ongoing behavioral decisions to continue exploring who our spouses are. But commitment is basically a decision; it doesn't have the emotion that intimacy and passion have. However, it is an equally important piece in understanding love.

There are basically two decisions involved with commitment. First is the decision to love, to make the commitment—to decide that we're going to get married for life! We can see clearly that this is a commitment and a decision. And then there is the ongoing decision we make regularly that we are going to *maintain and nurture* that love.

It's interesting to note that in cultures where marriages are arranged, there is no decision to love that leads to the marriage. We see this in *Fiddler on the Roof,* where Tevye sings the song that asks this question about his marriage: "Do I Love You?" Challenged by his children's desire to marry for love, he is confused by it all. Why don't they just accept the decision of the matchmaker? But as he grapples with this question, he goes through a list of loving behaviors he shares with his wife and that she shares with him, and they decide that yes, they do love each other. There was never a decision to love, but there was clearly the ongoing decision to act in loving ways, which represents the many long-term, ongoing decisions of commitment.

This commitment side of love is what gets us through the crisis times every couple will experience at some point in their marriage. It gets us through those inevitable times when the feelings of love are weak or even absent. It is what holds us together when "loving you" isn't easy. Without this ongoing decision to love, all too many couples give up and divorce, missing the lessons to be learned in the tough times. Most wedding vows are oriented toward the ongoing commitment part of marriage—for richer or poorer, in sickness and in health.

SECRET NO. 3:

Know That Love Has Three Facets: Intimacy, Passion, and Commitment

Couples who experience great marriages know the full scope of what love is and work at the ongoing preservation and development of intimacy, passion, and commitment. They know that these facets of love are developed not by happenstance but by consistently demonstrating the behaviors that keep the full range of love alive in the marriage.

THE BEHAVIORS OF LOVE

In his ministry on earth, Jesus Christ said, "This is my commandment: Love each other in the same way I have loved you" (John 15:12). Have you ever wondered how he could command an emotion? He goes on to describe to us how that love is experienced: "There is no greater love than to lay down one's life for one's friends." (John 15:13). What Jesus commands are the behaviors of love.

And have you ever noticed that in the great love chapter of the Bible—1 Corinthians 13—no emotion is even mentioned? All Paul says about love is behavioral!

"Love is patient and kind. Love is not jealous or boastful or proud or rude. It does not demand its own way. It is not irritable, and it keeps no record of being wronged. It does not rejoice about injustice but rejoices whenever the truth wins out. Love never gives up, never loses faith, is always hopeful, and endures through every circumstance" (1 Corinthians 13: 4–7).

Everything in this passage is a behavior. That's why love can be commanded—it is a behavior. And when the behaviors of love are active and present, the emotion and feelings of love are present as well.

We often talk with couples who tell us they no longer love their spouses. As we mentioned before, the problem here is that the behaviors of love have stopped. When those behaviors are absent, the feelings of love wither and die. But they can be resurrected! And it is done through the restoration of loving behaviors in the marriage.

The other complicating factor in expressing the behaviors of love is that the behaviors we often depend on to show love are the behaviors that *we* want. They aren't necessarily the behaviors that are meaningful to our spouses.

Whenever we suggest that a husband and wife write out 10 things the other person could do to show love and caring, one spouse (most often the wife) usually says, "If I have to tell him what to do, it spoils it for me. I just want him to do it without being told." We have to carefully point out that wanting him to do it without being told is usually a wish carried over from childhood when we wanted to be loved perfectly. In this situation it is far better to be loved imperfectly than to struggle with the feelings of not being loved at all.

Components of Love

The behaviors of love are made up of three components that make
them effective.

First, they have to be positive behaviors. They have to be things we
choose to *do*, not things that we stop doing. You may temporarily stop a
behavior because you forget or you're too tired. Stopping doesn't have
the same willfulness to it as actively choosing to do a positive behavior.

*Second, our description of the positive behavior needs to be concrete
and observable.* For example we often hear a wife say she wants her
husband to be more understanding. That's positive but abstract. How does
her husband show that behavior? And if he does act in some way that
communicates "understanding" to his wife, how will he know he is doing
it? We need behaviors that can be acted upon and be observable.

*Third, we need to do small, positive, concrete behaviors so they can be
repeated on a regular basis.* One woman put on her list "send me some
flowers." Her husband bought several long-stem roses for her and added
a creative touch. He hid them in the extra refrigerator in the garage and
each morning for several days placed a rose on the steering wheel of her
car. That represented a small, repeatable, concrete behavior that expressed
love in a way that was meaningful to her.

If you have trouble thinking of what your spouse could do for you,
think back to what he or she did for you that felt so good when you were
courting each other. Often those early behaviors eventually lose their
rewarding value and then gradually go away. It may be time to revive
them. You can also include on your list some of the things your spouse
is doing that you wish he or she would do more frequently.

CONCLUSION

Couples in great marriages have found ways to know what behaviors are meaningful to their spouses. They consistently continue to show their spouses the behaviors that lead to greater intimacy, that keep passion alive, and that underscore the continuing commitment to the marriage. They practice these behaviors and work at new and meaningful ways to continue to act on these behaviors. When the feelings of love run low, they automatically step up the behaviors of love. When stressors make extra demands on their time, they still find ways to connect. Because they have dealt with their basic fears, there are no taboo subjects in their relationship that close them off from each other. They not only know love, they know how to act lovingly.

So let's look at some of the ways you can better identify and express the behaviors of love in your marriage.

1 Robert J. Sternberg, *The Triangle of Love: Intimacy, Passion, Commitment* (New York: Basic Books, 1988), 284.

2 C. S. Lewis, *Mere Christianity* (New York: Macmillan, 1952), 115.

3 Michael and Karen Sytsma, "Keeping Passion Alive," *The Complete Marriage Book,* David and Jan Stoop, eds. (Grand Rapids, MI: Fleming H. Revell, 2002), 283–295.

CHAPTER SEVEN

From Feeling Love To Real Love

The Bible, the foundation of Western civilization and of Judeo-Christian society, does not describe love as a feeling. Its timeless Scriptures refer to love as a *behavior*. If we look at love as being based on certain behaviors, we can better understand the three sides of love identified in the previous chapter: intimacy, passion, and commitment. Our discussion of love behaviors should identify concrete things we can do to reinforce the three facets of love.

Guidelines for Exercises

The exercises in this chapter have heavy questions to discuss, so it is important to follow the guidelines concerning how to talk about them together. Follow these directions carefully:

- Decide who will go first.
- The one listening should close his or her eyes and must not interrupt.
- Slowly go through each statement, waiting after you finish each one before going on to the next.
- When you have finished all six statements, repeat this exercise, reversing roles.
- Review chapter 2 on listening and focus on hearing each other.
- It is important to listen to each other. You do not need to defend or explain or agree on any of these issues. One spouse may feel strongly positive about a response while the other person may not be so positive.
- Don't criticize what your spouse says or feels and work hard at not defending yourself.
- Seek to understand.
- Sit opposite each other and hold hands while you talk. Whatever you do, don't let go!

INVENTORY OF INTIMACY

Exercise 1

Begin by looking at the behaviors of intimacy. Get together with your spouse, set aside about 30 minutes, and discuss together the following four statements:

1. **We can count on each other in a time of need.** Give specific examples of when you were there for your spouse and one example of when you failed.

2. **We feel valued by the other person.** Describe the behaviors that support this statement.

3. **We each feel that the other person understands us.** How do you know you are understood?

4. **We feel trust with each other.** Describe ways in which you trust and some areas where you still need to work on trust.

Exercise 2

At another time work individually and privately. Write out how you would complete the following sentences:

1. I have felt pleasure and joy in our marriage when _____

_____

_____.

2. I have been irritated in our marriage about _____

_____

_____.

3. I get anxious when _____

_____

_____.

4. I feel sad when I think about _____

_____

_____.

5. I struggle with my emotions when _____

_____

_____.

6. What I like about our level of intimacy is _____

_____

_____.

Once you have finished each sentence, set a time when you can share with each other what you have written. Again follow the guidelines listed on page 97.

INVENTORY OF PASSION

Michael and Karen Systma give the following suggestions for keeping passion alive over the course of a marriage:[1]

- *First, stay focused on what is great in your marriage.* Follow the apostle Paul's advice: "Fix your thoughts on what is true, and honorable, and right, and pure, and lovely, and admirable. Think about things that are excellent and worthy of praise" (Philippians 4:8). It is all too easy to begin to zero in on the "weeds" in a marriage "garden" and forget the "flowers." Celebrate your spouse's beauty, skills, talents, and uniqueness.

- *Give grace to your partner.* Think the best of his or her intentions. We all have parts of ourselves that we are embarrassed about — parts that are unacceptable even to ourselves. That means your spouse has some "unacceptable" parts as well. To keep passion alive, it helps to think through the idea that every weakness has its hidden strength. An attitude of grace and ongoing forgiveness needs to be an ongoing part of your marriage relationship.

- *Give up your fantasies about how your marriage "should be."* One of the characteristics of a great marriage is that the expectations each spouse has for the other are close to the realities of the relationship. It is your perception of how your partner feels that is important, and the closer your perception is to reality, the stronger the marriage. You keep passion alive by seeing your partner more realistically.

- *Make your time together as a couple sacred.* That means there is nothing that can disrupt your time together. For years we set aside every Friday morning for our time together. We would go to a restaurant at the beach for breakfast and stay there with each other for two or three hours. It was "our time," and few things were ever important enough to cancel our Friday morning breakfasts. Our only agenda was to be there for each other. Now that our kids are grown, we meet three or four times a week at a restaurant for lunch with the same agenda.

- *Find ways to be playful with each other.* In the last chapter, we looked at play intimacy. This is an important aspect of our relationships as it is an important part of keeping passion alive.

- *And finally, dream together.* When you first married, you shared your dreams together. Over time many couples give up on their dreams, settling for the realities of the day-to-day demands of family. But those who still feel passion together still dream together. You're never too old to have a mutual dream for the future.

Exercise 3

Let's start inventorying what this passion facet of love looks like in your marriage. Discuss together the following six statements:

1. **We think about each other throughout the day.** Give examples.

2. **We would rather be with each other than with anyone else.** Discuss how that is true and why.

3. **We still find each other to be physically attractive.**

4. **We enjoy doing romantic things together.** Give examples.

5. **We are concerned about meeting each other's needs.** Give some examples of needs that are being met in your relationship. Then discuss some needs that aren't being met to the degree you would like.

6. **We know how to play together.** Talk about the things you do together that are fun.

Exercise 4

Playing together also keeps passion alive, as the Sytsmas point out. With all of modern life's pressures though, it's not easy to keep this part of marriage vibrant. Sometimes when we think of play, we think of all the other millions of things that demand our attention that are more "worthy" of our time.

Yet play is really an investment in your marriage. It is important that you carve out time to have fun together. Individually go through the following two steps. Then set a time when you can share with your spouse what you have written.

1. **Make a list of fun things you enjoy.** Remember what fun was for you as a child. Fun doesn't have to be practical. And there is nothing that you can put on your list that is wrong. Do not consider financial issues or time constraints. Just let yourself dream and write it down.

2. **Think about what keeps you from having fun together.** What are the stressors in your life together that rob you of fun? Write them down. What are the attitudes you have that limit your ability to have fun? Do you think fun is childish? Is life too serious to waste time? Is work too important to allow time for fun? Write out your thoughts to these questions.

When finished review each other's lists. Choose several fun things that you agree on. Then look at what attitudes and circumstances keep you from having fun together. What changes do you need to make to carve out some time for "passionate" fun together?

INVENTORY OF COMMITMENT

Exercise 5

Discuss together your responses to the following statements. Remember to abide by the guidelines at the beginning of the chapter.

1. **We are committed to maintaining our marriage relationship.**
   Describe some ways you show this commitment.

2. **We are confident in the stability of our marriage.** Describe evidence of this confidence.

3. **We feel a strong sense of responsibility for our marriage.** How do your actions illustrate this?

4. **We believe in the sanctity of our marriage vows.** Talk together about what you remember saying in your vows.

5. **We know we are solidly committed to each other, even during difficult times.** Discuss how you know this.

6. **We see ourselves renewing our vows together on a regular basis.** Talk about how you do, or could do, this.

COMBINATIONS OF LOVE

It's interesting to look at the three aspects of love (intimacy, passion, commitment) we learned about in the previous chapter and see what happens when they're combined in various ways. There are seven possible scenarios.

When we fall into experiencing only one type of love, we lose the depth marriage was intended to have. Read through the following descriptions and assess where you are in expressing love.

Intimacy Alone

What if all we have in our love is intimacy—no passion and no commitment? When this occurs we have the experience of liking someone.

You may feel a strong sense of intimacy with close friends in that they know a lot about you. You may feel close to them and feel warmth in the relationship. But intimacy alone leads eventually only to liking someone. There is no passion and no conscious commitment.

Passion Alone

When all we have is romantic passion, we call it infatuation. This is what we felt as teenagers in that first experience of what our parents called "puppy love."

Sweaty palms, heart palpitations, and stomach jitters are often experienced when someone is fascinated with the idea of being with another person. It was real to us, but it lacked intimacy—there was no knowing of each other—and it lacked commitment. The passionate feelings of romanticized passion would eventually wear off, and often we would even feel an aversion to the person we had been so "madly in love with" just a short time before. Romanticized passion alone doesn't last over time.

Commitment Alone

This is a very empty form of love. We have a neighbor whose marriage reflected commitment alone. The couple was married for almost 60 years, but there was no sense of intimacy or passion in their marriage. In fact, when the wife died, the husband was very open about his hatred of her. But they were committed!

Sometimes this is the final aspect of love in a marriage that is about to dissolve. The intimacy is long gone, and the passion is long forgotten. And when commitment dies, divorce follows.

Intimacy + Passion

This is what romantic love is all about. This is one form of "Hollywood" love. It is what we see in the movies and read about in romance novels.

Basically this consists of liking a person and adding passion to the equation, which leads to sleeping together with no strings attached. There is a physical attraction that draws the two people together, but their lack of commitment doesn't keep them together. Sometimes the couple marries, but the commitment is short lived. When the passion dies, the commitment to the marriage dies as well.

Intimacy + Commitment

This is what couples in good-enough marriages often settle for. The passion is gone, but they still share a long-term, committed friendship. Many of these couples have survived the tough times and consider themselves to be the best of friends. The union falls short of a great marriage because of the lack of passion for each other.

Passion + Commitment

This is another form of "Hollywood" love; we might say it's the *People* magazine form of love. The couple makes a commitment and marries, but they don't take the time to really develop intimacy—to really get to know each other. The couple meets on a movie set, the magazines are full of reports of their "romance," and a few weeks later they are married—that is unless they first have to get out of their current marriages. These couples commit themselves to each other on the basis of passion, which cannot sustain a relationship.

Intimacy + Passion + Commitment

Here is the definition of real love. It is a complete love, as all three components of love are present. It is the kind of love that those in great marriages are able to experience.

We experience this kind of love in our parent-child relationships, which is often why—when one of the components is missing in the marriage—one spouse is jealous of the attention given to the child. We know our children at a deep level. We are involved in the motivational needs of the child, which is a part of passion, and we are committed to our children. Most of us find it easy to love our children in this way as they are growing up.

A married couple can also love each other in this way, and when they do they have an important ingredient of a great marriage.

ACTING OUT REAL LOVE

We described in the last chapter how the behaviors of love have to be meaningful to each spouse, or else he or she will not be impacted by those behaviors. The following exercise will help you discover meaningful boundaries.

Exercise 6

In all of our seminars, we give a homework assignment for each person to create a "care-giving list" to help their spouse understand what behaviors are meaningful. Separately take the time to do this now.

Make a list of 10 things that your spouse could or already does do for you that shows he or she cares. Each thing on your list must be:

- Positive—something your partner could or does choose to do.
- Concrete—something someone could observe.
- Repeatable—small enough that it could be repeated each day.

1. _____
   _____

2. _____
   _____

3. _____
   _____

4. _____
   _____

5. _____
   _____

6. _____
   _____

7. _____
   _____

8. _____
   _____

9. _____
   _____

10. _____
    _____

Once you make your list, exchange it with your spouse and do any one thing from your spouse's list each day for the next 30 days. When your partner does something from your list, acknowledge it and express thanks for caring. You might want to mark your calendar and repeat this process with a new list every six months.

A Word for Men

Men often have a difficult time coming up with 10 things for their lists. It is important to be creative about this. Put in some effort. Get help from other men. Ask them what their wives do for them that feels good. Don't be afraid to be vulnerable in making your list.

Be romantic but don't make everything sexual. Think of things like a back rub, a favorite meal or dessert, a call at the office, a note in your suitcase, picking up your cleaning, watching a sport with you, and so on. Whatever you, *do not* dismiss this by saying that your wife is already doing everything without identifying what she does. That will feel dismissive to her and undo the connectedness you are trying to build.

A Word for Women

It seems it's a little easier for women to come up with things to put on the list. But be careful to not include things that you have had "discussions" about in the past—in other words, things that have been hurtful or painful in your relationship. Try to think up new things that you would like him to do. Remember that your asking doesn't take away from its value or meaning.

A FINAL THOUGHT ON LOVE

To conclude this chapter, ponder these powerful words from C. S. Lewis, the famous British Christian apologist and writer:

> To love at all is to be vulnerable. Love anything, and your heart will certainly be wrung and possibly be broken. If you want to make sure of keeping it intact, you must give your heart to no one, not even to an animal. Wrap it carefully round with hobbies and little luxuries; avoid all entanglements; lock it up safe in the casket or coffin of your selfishness. But in that casket—safe, dark, motionless, airless—it will change. It will not be broken; it will become unbreakable, impenetrable, irredeemable. The alternative to tragedy, or at least to the risk of tragedy, is damnation. The only place outside Heaven where you can be perfectly safe from all the dangers and perturbations of love is Hell.[2]

1 *The Complete Marriage Book,* David and Jan Stoop, eds. (Grand Rapids, MI: Fleming H. Revell, 2002).

2 C. S. Lewis, *The Four Loves* (New York: Harcourt Brace Jovanovich, 1960), 169.

CHAPTER EIGHT

The Question of Leadership

Wife: "We'd have a great marriage
if only I didn't have to initiate everything."

Leadership in a good-enough marriage can have either the man in charge or the woman in charge. As counselors we've seen examples of both. We've also seen good-enough marriages where it would seem to an outside observer that no one was in charge. In these marriages the couple has worked out an arrangement regarding leadership that is satisfying to both—and that works. As we will see in this chapter, this is not the case in great marriages.

I remember seeing a coffee mug that pictures a group of people on one side, and on the other side there was a confused-looking man saying, "Where are they? Which way did they go? I'm their leader." That seems to be the common experience of men when they are confronted with the question of leadership in the home and in marriage.

Tim and Adrianne were in the second year of their marriage when they came in for help. As they sat down on the couch, it was obvious they were nervous about having to be in my office. We exchanged some pleasantries to help relax the situation, and then I (Dave) asked, "What brings you to counseling?" After a few minutes of silence, Tim finally said, "Well, the problem is with my wife. She won't let me be the leader in our marriage."

I waited, and Tim continued, "She wants me to be the leader in our marriage, but every time I try to lead, she is either critical of how I am doing something, or she just doesn't want to do what I suggest."

As we talked about their problem, it became increasingly clear that neither Tim nor Adrianne knew what was involved in Tim being the "leader."

WHO'S IN CHARGE?

Tim and Adrianne's dilemma represents the struggle a lot of couples face in the early years of their marriages—the question of leadership. Who's going to be in charge of what? In their case the question had stirred up a major crisis with a lot of painful misunderstandings. In contrast some couples simply accept the fact that the wife runs everything with the husband just settling in with a passive attitude.

An old story tells about a man who described his marriage by saying that his wife made all the little decisions and he made all the big ones. When asked what some examples of the big decisions were, he said, "Oh, like 'Should we go to war?' or 'What are we going to do about the national deficit?' Things like that." Obviously his wife ran the marriage and he had accepted the fact that she was in charge.

Tim wasn't about to settle for that arrangement. He could only think of what his wife wouldn't let him do. The irony of his position was that he did not realize that in the struggle he was really setting his own leadership style by ceding leadership to his wife. He thought she was the one who determined what kind of leader he was being.

In all my years as a pastor and as a psychologist, I don't ever remember a husband asking me the question, "How do I lead?" Even Tim wasn't really asking that question.

As we counsel couples, we often observe the subtle power position of a woman who is urging her husband to be the leader of their home. She says to him, "I want you to be the leader of this marriage and to take your role as leader seriously!" So isn't she the one in the position of power—

the leader—as she seeks to determine who the leader will be? Isn't whoever gets to pick the leader really the leader? Maybe not. Let's look at it.

WHAT ABOUT "HEADSHIP"?

David Blankenhorn tells of an experience he had while in Chicago.[2] He was interviewing a number of African American women who were members of the Apostolic Church of God. He asked them if their husbands were the heads of their families. They all agreed that the husbands were. Then he asked what that meant. He said the women were "equally united and emphatic" in their answer. To them it meant three things: the husband worked hard to support the family financially, he led the family in prayer, and he took the family to church on Sundays.

Then Blankenhorn asked, "Aren't you equally capable of leadership in your families?" And they smiled as they agreed that they definitely were capable. But they went on to point out that when their husbands did these things, it made a difference in their families. It was as if the men had made a choice, as if somehow they knew the consequences of not leading. They could either take the leadership in their marriages and families, or they could end up turning to drugs, then going to prison, and ultimately meeting an early death. They believed that when the husbands led, the families thrived and survived. If the husbands didn't lead, the family would break down and the husbands would likely wander away and end up in trouble.

CALLED TO LEAD

When one turns to the pages of the Bible, it is easy to agree with these women. The man is called to be the leader of his family. 1 Corinthians 11:3 says it clearly: "Now I want you to realize that the head of every man is Christ, and the head of the woman is man, and the head of Christ is God" (NIV). This concept is established in Genesis 2:20–24, where in the order of creation, man is first. Then woman was made from man and the man gave her name—both symbols of leadership.

All of this changed with the Fall. When Adam and Eve sinned, one of the consequences was that men, left to their own sinful propensities, would seek to dominate women, and women, left to their own sinful propensities, would seek to undermine and rebel against men.[1] But because of what Jesus Christ demonstrated, as the perfect example of a servant leader, we can overcome this curse. Because we live on this side of the cross, marriage can move beyond the consequences of the fall, and we can choose to be equal partners with each other.

The original design in Genesis 1:27, 28 as well as in Genesis 2 conveys the truth that man and woman are equals. Both are made in the image of God. And it is implied that when Adam was created, he was complete in himself. God didn't make woman the same way he made man. And when God took a part out of Adam to make the woman, Adam was now incomplete, and so was the woman. Their completion, and ours, can only come through the experience of oneness in marriage. Oneness restores a sense of wholeness to both the man and the woman.

HOW HEADSHIP LOOKS IN MARRIAGE

There are several principles here for marriage. First, we must always affirm that the husband and wife are equals. Neither is less than the other! Second, there is a complementary relationship between a husband and wife. The husband is incomplete without the wife, and the wife is incomplete without the husband. And this complementariness also implies the surrender of self in love. And that surrender to one another leads to oneness. And third, the man is the "source" of the woman. She is taken out of him. What she is comes from the man. Some take this to mean that the man is superior to the woman, but that is not the meaning here. Keep in mind the phrase "what she is comes from the man." We'll look at the meaning of the man being the "source" a little later.

What we can say is this: There is a greater responsibility for the husband. Look at the famous "submission" passage in Ephesians 5:21–32. There are about 60 words in that passage that describe the role of the wife, but there are about 120 words that describe what the husband is to do. He is not told just to love his wife, but he is to "love his wife just as Christ loved the church."

How does Christ love the church? For an answer to that question, look at Philippians 2:5–11. In that passage we read that Christ loves the church so much he is willing to give up his rights; he humbles himself as a slave; and he obediently dies a criminal's death.

That's a powerful yet submissive form of love that goes far beyond what is expected of the woman. It is also why Ephesians 5:21 can say we are to submit to each other in reverence to Christ. Our oneness comes from this mutual submission.

SECRET NO. 4:

Husbands Lead

In great marriages the man willingly takes the role of leadership in the marriage. It is the man who sets the pace for a truly great marriage.

One of the findings of research into why marriages succeed focused on the role of the husband. John Gottman found that when a husband rejected the influence of his wife, the marriage was doomed to failure. When the husband allowed himself to be influenced by his wife, it was a high predictor of marital success. On the other hand, whether the wife rejected or accepted the influence of the husband, predicted nothing. For whatever the reasons there is something here that is extremely important—when a man listens to and validates his wife, something powerful happens.[3]

In his research Gottman found there was a large variability in how men responded to their wives. And how they responded to their wives was highly predictive of the outcome of the marriage.

Marriages become great when the man accepts his wife's influence— when he communicates to her that she and her opinions are valued. This accepting of the wife's influence does not mean that the man complies with everything his wife says. This is man's greatest fear—that his wife will dominate him and he will be seen as a wimp. What it does mean is that the man communicates to his wife that she is an equal partner and has wisdom that God has given her. It also means that the husband stands his ground on some issues and yields ground on other issues.

In other words the research backs up what the Bible says about headship—*the man sets the pace in the marriage.* If he is open to his wife, knows how to validate her ideas and opinions, and gives value to her, his behavior *alone* is a high predictor of the quality of the marriage the couple will enjoy! The secret of a great marriage is that the man leads in such a way that he is the one who creates the environment for greatness!

THE HUSBAND AS THE "SOURCE"

When we think of "headship" as a call to leadership, we can recognize this principle as being active in all sorts of places. For example the CEO of a company sets the pace and creates the corporate environment. The headmaster of a school creates the image of that school in the minds of the parents and students. The leader is the one to establish the overall environment and temperament of the relationship.

One way to think about headship, or leadership, is to liken it to the term "headwaters." A television documentary some years ago recounted the search for the headwaters of the mighty Amazon River. The search team followed small streams up into the Andes Mountains to come to the source of that great river. Everything that river is comes from its sources— those little streams high in the Andes Mountains.

What happens if we think of the man's role in the marriage as being the "source" for all that goes on in the marriage? I've interacted with a number of men on this point. And as I have talked with them, I have pointed out that headship is not an option—it is a fact that is always in operation. The man is *already* the one who is setting the pace for the marriage. He is *already* the source of what is going on in the marriage. I tell them, "You set the pace whether you intend to or not. You are ultimately responsible for what is going right and what is going wrong in your marriage." What the wife is in the marriage comes from the man, for the woman came from the man.

Another couple, John and Marge, faced the same issue from a different side. John argued continually with me about this. He couldn't see that he was setting the pace in his marriage. He was quick to point out that their real problem was his wife's anger. "She criticizes everything I do. And she gets even angrier with me when I don't do anything in an attempt to try and avoid her criticism. How am I setting the pace in that?" he asked. Then he added, "She's just always angry regardless of what I do or don't do. Why don't you work on her?"

As the three of us talked together, I could see that he was right—Marge was very angry with him. It was a deep-seated anger that she had felt for a number of years. But as we talked, it became clear that what was behind her anger was a deep hurt. She was convinced that John didn't really care about her or even love her. And every time she said this, he reiterated his love for her.

"How can you say that?" he would ask. "You know I love you."

"No, I don't," Marge would retort.

And on and on it would go. As we talked, I stepped in to point out to John that it was clear that nothing that was important to Marge was even on John's radar screen. In fact Marge said that it even felt like if something was important to her, John purposely avoided even acknowledging it, let alone ever talking to her about it.

I turned to John and asked him if he knew what was important to Marge. He nodded. He could list things because he'd heard them many times. As he and I talked, it seemed that what he struggled with was this:

If he did what Marge wanted, he would lose his identity—he would become a henpecked wimp. So he was determined to ignore Marge's requests. "Well I don't really ignore what she says. I just try to determine to do things my way and in my time," he added.

I was candid with John and let him know that he was setting the pace in the marriage with his attitude. Whether he knew it or not, whatever he chose to do or not do was seen by Marge as setting the pace. I said, "You're the 'source' whether you want to be or not."

"Oh no I'm not," he was quick to jump in and say. "She runs everything. If it's not done her way, I'm in trouble. I have no say in what goes on in our marriage!"

"I know it feels that way to you," I responded, "but what I'm trying to get you to see is that you are the source. That's just the way it works. And therefore you can change the tone in the marriage by at least changing your attitude." Then I added, "I wonder what would happen if you were to make what is important to Marge important to you?"

Look at it this way. Go back to 1 Corinthians 11:3 and read it like this: "But there is one thing I want you to know: The *source* of every man is Christ, the *source* of every woman is man, and the *source* of Christ is God." Do you see how that fits? And what is so interesting is that recent research into what makes marriages succeed points to the man as the source—he is the one who sets the pace for success.

One of the ways a husband can change the tone of the marriage is to identify what is important to his wife. John knew what his wife wanted and needed from him. When a husband knows this, the whole relationship will change for the better. Once John understood that the things Marge was saying were important to her and were really the things she used to determine whether or not he cared about her and their marriage, he eventually shifted gears and started to take the initiative in doing some of those things. He appeared surprised as he reported to me that Marge had seemed much less critical and that the atmosphere of their marriage was improving.

Reflect on marriages that you feel are healthy. Do you see evidence of the wife and husband respecting what is important to one another? You may also want to note what is really important to your spouse and how you show that you value him or her as well.

A wife can be an encourager, giving her husband the room to work on being the "source" and leaning lightly on him when he fails or sinks back into old ways. Be especially careful to avoid criticizing the husband, as that will only reinforce the old patterns. Remember also that the husband typically starts out in marriage a few steps behind the wife when it comes to understanding how relationships work. Patience and encouragement are two important qualities for the wife to exhibit as her husband works on setting a better pace for the marriage.

CONCLUSION

Perhaps it's time for all of us to put the discussion about submission on the shelf for a while and focus on what the man can do in being the source for his wife. What I've found over the years is that in couples that experience great marriages, the husband sets the pace for greatness. He has recognized that he is the one who, by his attitudes and involvements, creates the environment that leads to greatness. He doesn't get all caught up in issues of leadership and the wife's role—he recognizes that he is the source for sets a pace that leads to a relationship that is constantly growing. In the next chapter, we'll look specifically at the things a husband can do in the marriage that will lead to greatness.

1 See Genesis 3:16, where God says to Eve, "And you will desire to control your husband, but he will rule over you."

2 David Blankenhorn, Don Browning, and Mary Stewart Van Leeuwen, eds., *Does Christianity Teach Male Headship?* (Grand Rapids, MI: Eerdmans, 2004).

3 John M. Gottman, *Marital Therapy: A Research-Based Approach,* Clinicians Manual, (Seattle, WA: The Gottman Institute, 2000).

Where Are They? Which Way Did They Go? I'm Their Leader.

CHAPTER NINE

We've met a lot of men like Tim and John. They believe they have no say in their marriages—that their wives run everything. And like Tim and John, they cannot see that they are the ones who determine the patterns in their marriages. A husband can set the pace from passivity. When he fails to see his role and responsibility, the health of the marriage is jeopardized. When we have confronted husbands on this point, they usually say, "I don't know what to do." To help them see the dynamic more accurately, we like to take them out of the marriage context and ask them some questions about their jobs.

It amazes many of them to realize they already have most of the tools they need to change the pace in their marriages. We ask them if at work they know how to set priorities. Of course they do. We ask them if they know how to set goals for themselves on the job. They answer in the affirmative. Then we ask them if they can focus on reaching their goals. And again they answer in the affirmative. What about negotiating? And how about handling conflicts and resolving issues between workers? Most men say they know how to do all of these things on the job.

Then we ask why they don't use these same tools to improve their marriage relationships. And they usually give us a look of surprise. No one had ever suggested the parallel to them.

SETTING THE PACE

So what's a husband to do? How can he effectively set a healthy pace for the marriage? He can start by prioritizing what is important to his wife in their relationship. Then he can set some goals, focus on those goals, strategize on how to reach them, negotiate what needs to be negotiated, and use the skills he already has to work through the conflicts. There are also some important things he needs to understand in order to be the husband he wants to be in the marriage. Following are four things he needs to understand:

1. Understand and Accept Strengths and Weaknesses

First, a husband needs to understand himself. That involves accurately assessing his strengths and his weaknesses. Setting the pace in your marriage does not mean you have to take care of everything. There are some things in a marriage relationship that husbands need to avoid and let their wives take care of.

For example some men have difficulty paying their bills on time. They are too busy with other things, don't like the routine of bill paying, or are too absentminded to keep their credit scores above 700. That would be an area of weakness one could identify. So as a part of leading well, a husband needs to see that if bill paying is one of the strengths of his wife, he should let her have the job. If neither husband nor wife is good at staying ahead of the bills, they need either someone else to help them or some automatic bill-paying system on their computer. The important thing is to not pretend to have a skill you don't have. A husband and wife should learn how to be good stewards of one another's strengths, allowing those strengths to benefit the marriage.

There is a difference between skills and roles. This means we give up the idea that some jobs in a marriage automatically belong to the man and some automatically belong to the woman. That can be a recipe for disaster in some marriages. So part of how the man sets the pace is by knowing what he's good at and what he's not good at, and tasks are defined by skill level, not by male-female roles.

We have friends who divide their tasks like this so the wife does many of the typical male tasks. She paints the walls, builds things for the house, arranges for the contractors—all so-called "man of the house" tasks. She does them well, and her husband isn't threatened by his lack of skill in those areas. He gladly gives her the freedom to use the natural abilities God placed in her.

Another couple we know handles tasks in another manner. The husband does all the cooking and meal planning. He loves to cook, and his wife is happy to let him. Her job is to clean up the mess he makes while cooking and to do the dishes. Not the typical division of duties in a marriage, but it works wonderfully.

Take a minute now and look at the various tasks in running your marriage and home.

• What are some "male" tasks the wife is doing? List them here.

_____

_____

_____

_____

_____

_____

_____

_____

_____

_____

_____

• What are some of the "female" tasks the husband is doing? List
  them here.

_____

_____

_____

_____

_____

_____

_____

_____

_____

_____

• What are some tasks you are each doing that fit the stereotypical
  roles in a marriage? List them here.

_____

_____

_____

_____

_____

_____

_____

_____

_____

_____

After you have made your lists, discuss how you divided up the different tasks. Then talk about the tasks you are each doing that do not reflect your strengths. What changes could you make to this group of tasks? Discuss if you are comfortable with all the tasks on your list and what could change to alter the list and make the marriage stronger.

2. Learn How Your Past Still Affects Your Present

Second, men have to take the time to look back at how the issues related to their families-of-origin still influence their present behaviors. There is an old proverb that states, "There are six people in the marriage bed." The six are the couple along with both sets of parents. Perhaps today, with divorces and remarriage and generations living longer, we need to say there are at least six people, perhaps eight, ten, or more people in the marriage bed.

What this saying refers to is the impact our parents' marriages have on shaping our current marriage relationships. Men, it seems, have a difficult time believing that our past can have a powerful influence on how we live in the present. The truth is that whatever issues we haven't resolved in our past are, in all likelihood, still influencing our behaviors in the present.

Probably the most significant relationship men struggle with in their past is with their fathers. Ever since the Industrial Revolution when fathers were taken off the homestead to work in the factory, sons and daughters lost contact with their fathers. This has had an effect on both men and women—women regarding the type of man they choose to marry and men regarding what it means to be a man, a father, and especially a husband.

Take some time now to talk together about what your father was like for you as you were growing up. First, discuss together some of the things you admire about your father. Discuss the following questions:

- **For the husband:** What are some of the ways you wanted to be like your father, and what are some of the ways you wanted to be different from your father?

_____

_____

_____

_____

_____

_____

_____

_____

_____

- **For the wife:** What are some of the ways you wanted your husband to be like your father, and what are some of the ways you wanted your husband to be different from your father?

_____

_____

_____

_____

_____

_____

_____

_____

Of course mothers have also had a strong influence on who we are and what kind of spouses we are in marriage. The old song said, "I want a gal just like the gal that married dear old Dad." We don't all feel that way, but that doesn't minimize the influence our mothers have on our marriages. First, discuss some of the things you admire about your mothers. Then discuss the following questions:

- **For the husband:** What are some of the ways you wanted your wife to be like your mother, and what are some of the ways you wanted your wife to be different from your mother?

  _____

  _____

  _____

  _____

  _____

  _____

  _____

  _____

- **For the wife:** What are some of the ways you wanted to be like your mother, and what are some of the ways you wanted to be different from your mother?

  _____

  _____

  _____

  _____

  _____

  _____

Don't be discouraged if you find that in many ways you are becoming like the parent you didn't want to be. All too often this happens because we only look at what we don't want and never really define what we do want. Finish your conversation on this subject by taking any negatives you have stated and restate them in terms of what positive behaviors you want to express. This is especially important for the husband. Grappling more with what you *do* want will help you move out of unwanted patterns.

3. Become Comfortable in the Land of Emotions

Third, if the husband is going to set a good pace for the marriage, he must become comfortable in the land of emotions. There is a cartoon in which the wife is trying to access her husband's emotions. Suddenly he is transported to a strange new world. When he asks where he is, the wife says, "You are in the land of emotions." It can be a strange new world to many men, but it doesn't have to remain strange.

Part of the problem for men is that they have avoided the land of emotions for most of their lives. As boys on the playground, they didn't sit around and talk about what they were feeling; they played hard and competed. As teens, being emotional was not in the mix of how boys socialized with their peers, so they continued to stay away from the land of emotions. Then men get married, and their wives are surprised by their discomfort with emotions. After all a man does try to be somewhat emotional while courting his future wife. But once married he retreats again into his comfort zone far away from the land of emotions.

If the husband is going to set a pace that leads to a great marriage, however, he must become comfortable with his and his wife's emotions. Sometimes he needs to learn the vocabulary of emotions. I (Dave) remember asking a very nonemotional man what he was feeling in regard to something his wife had just said. He started by saying, "Well, I think …" and I cut him off. I repeated again that I wanted to know what he was feeling. He sat there silently, unable to describe his feelings.

So I asked him a series of questions, each question framed around a particular emotion. It was interesting that he was able to respond to the question with a "yes" or "no" when the emotion was given a descriptive word. He knew what he was feeling; he just didn't have the vocabulary to describe it. Part of what I was doing was showing his wife that he had feelings and emotions, but he had no language with which to describe what he was feeling. Sometimes this scenario is in reverse; the wife does not know how to articulate what she is feeling and the man does.

In the case above, the husband was a very analytical engineer and was very bright. So I gave both him and his wife the following assignment: "Every time you see a look on your wife's face that you don't understand, I want you to ask her what she is feeling. And I want you to analyze the look on her face and match it with the feeling she is identifying." I went on to explain that this was to be a long-term learning process for him. He was eager to begin his analysis of his wife's emotions, and she agreed to help him learn the language of emotions.

Studies, in particular those by Paul Ekman,[1] have shown that across cultures—from primitive to advanced—the facial expression for each emotion we experience is universal. The facial expression of a woman in the the Amazon who is angry looks just like the angry wife in American suburbia. This is not just limited to anger; every emotion we experience will show on our faces and will look the same as anyone else on Earth. So if I study my wife's face and learn to identify the emotions behind the look, I will be educating myself on living in the land of emotions and will be able to identify the emotion behind the look on my boss' face as well.

Take some time to discuss this and practice feeling an emotion. Then analyze the look on each other's face at that time. Have some fun with it as you explore facial expressions as a key to understanding emotions.

4. Take the Initiative

Finally, the husband who wants to set a pace toward a great marriage needs to take the initiative in the things going on in the home, in the family, and in the marriage. Because he has adjusted his priorities and is now using his job-related skills at home as well, he can see ways in which he can take the initiative.

For example we've found that when couples pray together on a daily basis, incredible things begin to happen in their marriages. But often it is the wife who takes the initiative to start praying together or to remind her husband to pray with her. If the man is going to set the pace in the marriage, he needs to be the one who initiates praying together. And he needs to continue to do this until it becomes an established behavioral pattern.

Again, if there is a sudden financial problem, the husband needs to take the initiative to sit down and discuss the problem, not wait until it becomes a crisis or attempt to solve it quietly on his own. You can apply this same principle to parenting issues, in-law issues, church attendance issues, and so on. Rather than acting like a lot of men do who are not setting a good pace in their marriages, the husband who is building a great marriage is involved and lovingly initiates an issue in need of attention.

HUSBAND'S LEADERSHIP INVENTORY
IN AREAS OF INTIMACY

Husbands, let's take the eight areas of intimacy described in Chapter 5 and evaluate how well you are setting a pace for greatness. Rate yourself on how you see yourself taking the initiative in each area of intimacy. When you have finished, set a time to sit down with your wife and share with her your perceptions. She is *not* going to rate you on these scales, but she is to interact with you by giving her responses to your perceptions.

On a scale of 1 to 10, with 1 representing failure and 10 representing perfection, how would you rate yourself as setting a pace toward greatness in each area of intimacy?

1. Emotional Intimacy: _____
2. Physical Intimacy: _____
3. Conflict Intimacy: _____
4. Work Intimacy: _____
5. Intellectual Intimacy: _____
6. Creative Intimacy: _____
7. Play Intimacy: _____
8. Spiritual Intimacy: _____

Obviously no one will score all 10s, and your scores represent only your perceptions. When you have finished, share your perceptions with your wife and listen as she responds. Her perceptions will probably be different, but you are both right. Don't get into a discussion defending your scores. The purpose of this exercise is to identify areas of strength regarding how you set the pace and areas where you need to grow.

When you have finished the discussion of your ratings, talk about how you can better set the pace in those areas where you both agree you need to be more active.

The Passive Man

What happens when the husband is passive about setting the pace? This is a problem that we see quite often in working with couples. Tim, whom we met in the previous chapter, set a very passive pace for his marriage. And there are a lot of men who are just like Tim, at least to some degree. There is danger for the man when he sets a passive pace in that his wife will attempt to set the pace, and she will probably do it with lots of anger. But there are also three dangerous outcomes waiting to grab a passive man.

One, he's going to get stuck in either the emotion of fear or the emotion of anger. One might say that this is actually a cause of his failure to set a pace to greatness in the marriage, but typically it is more of a consequence. Like Tim and John, the man will react first with anger when his wife takes over and starts to lead the marriage relationship. In many cases his anger causes him to try to lord over his wife, and the ensuing power struggle will only add to the anger in both of them.

Over time, however, his anger will turn into fear. He will not only be afraid to change the pace he is setting in the marriage, he is fearful of his wife's anger. So he retreats in his fear, which obviously works against him as his wife's anger grows stronger over time and eventually leads him to become even more passive in the marriage.

A husband needs to recognize that a wife's continuing anger can be related to his passivity and his failure to set the pace in a positive, constructive way. Because his passivity is so powerful, the husband is the best one to break this cycle by stepping up to the plate and actively participating, which will in turn calm his wife.

A second dangerous outcome is that the husband who is passive about the pace and stride of the marriage often will turn all of his energy toward his work. He may not admit it, but greed fills the void left in his marriage, and he works himself to the bone to make as much money as possible. He gains his sense of value from knowing how much money he is making. He thinks more money will cool his wife's anger, and on the surface it does. With or without the extra money, she angrily spends it as fast or even faster than he can make it. But there isn't enough money in the world that can make up for a husband's failure to consciously set a pace to greatness in his marriage.

The third danger is that some men will withdraw from their pace-setting role in their marriages and turn instead to sexual perversions. For them strip clubs, magazines, or online pornography take the place of marital relationships. An addiction to online pornography is often directly correlated to a man's failure to take seriously his role in setting the pace in the marriage. When he gives up on this role in his marriage, he often numbs himself with pornography—a place where he thinks he has total control. Of course he will be very reluctant to admit that in reality he is out of control and is being controlled by his addiction.

Most men, when they are unaware of their role as the leader in their marriages, will turn to one or more of these dangerous diversions. In each case the husband fails to take seriously his role as the one to raise the bar in his marriage. Either he claims he doesn't know what to do, or he is in some way fearful of taking responsibility for change. But counseling and research prove that when the man takes seriously his role as a husband and is serious about setting the pace toward greatness, the wife is responsive—she's ready and waiting.

---

1 Paul Ekman, *Emotions Revealed* (New York: Henry Holt & Company, 2003).

The Whole Truth And Nothing But The Truth

CHAPTER TEN

"We could have a great marriage if my
wife were more open and honest with me."

It's not easy to tell the whole truth. Jim Carrey's character finds this out in the movie *Liar, Liar,* where he portrays a lawyer who often is too busy for his son. So for a birthday wish, his son wishes that it would be impossible for his father to tell a lie for a whole day. His wish is granted. There are some hilarious scenes, especially the ensuing chaos Carrey's character creates in the courtroom, which leads him to being jailed briefly. When you stop laughing, though, you realize how easy it is to lie and just how prevalent lying is in our culture.

In fact everyone lies. Parents lie to their children. They make up excuses for why the child can't do something, or why the parent can't do something for or with the child. We call them "excuses," when they really are lies. And children lie to their parents. Kids are very creative in their lies, sometimes so creative that their parents see right through them. Parents punish their children for lying, and, fortunately for parents, their children can't punish them.

Politicians are expected to lie, but we still vote for them. They tell us one thing during the election and then tell us something else after they are elected. Teachers lie to their students, and students lie to their teachers. We see cartoons about the lies students tell: "The dog ate my homework." Employers lie to their employees. "There's not enough money for bonuses this year," they claim, but they don't tell anyone that management is still getting theirs. Executives lie to their fellow executives. It's all a part of "getting ahead."

And employees lie to their employers. They were sick yesterday when in reality they were interviewing for another job. And employees lie to each other as well—"getting ahead" again.

And husbands lie to their wives and wives lie to their husbands. We're not talking about the big lies here, only the little ones. Like, "Oh, I've had this dress for ages," when in reality we bought it a few months ago and hid it until now. Or, "She doesn't need to know about the speeding ticket I got today. What she doesn't know won't hurt her." We typically think there's nothing really wrong with these "little white lies."

Advertisements sometimes give us new ideas about how to lie. "Why not rent a luxury car to drive to the high school reunion?" one ad suggested. Make your friends think you're really successful. In many ways our culture expects people to lie, and that's why *Liar, Liar,* in the midst of its humor, also shows us how in many situations lying is the only way to get along.

WHY DO WE LIE?

Our first lie was probably designed to protect us from punishment. I (Dave) remember one of my early lies. I was about seven years old and I had been told not to walk on the snow banks between the sidewalks and the streets because usually at the driveways the snow was a very wet slush. Well of course I did what I wasn't supposed to do, and I slipped and fell into the snow. Walking home in my cold, muddy clothes, I had time to think up an explanation (a lie). I was pushed by a big kid into a puddle.

I'm sure the guilty look on my face made my parents skeptical, but at least on the surface they bought my lie. And my success at avoiding punishment with that lie led to more lies in the future as a means of protecting myself from punishment.

Of course when my sister lied to protect herself at my expense, I was usually helpless to convince my parents of my truthfulness and her lack of truthfulness. I'm sure I set her up the same way—all as a means of avoiding punishment and protecting myself.

Protection

That's also why we adults lie: to protect ourselves. We lie to our bosses to protect our jobs. We lie to the cop to try and escape the traffic ticket. We lie to our kids because we don't want to take the time to explain the truth to them. We lie to our spouses because we don't want the hassle that the truth might cause.

Another reason we lie is to protect someone else. We may want to protect someone we care about because we know they would protect us. Or our protecting them is in some way protecting us. As kids we wanted to protect our parents from the truth of what we were doing or not doing. As adults we do the same thing. We lie to the boss so he or she won't get upset. We lie to our spouses because we don't want them to get upset. We really are protecting them from the pain we think the truth could possibly bring.

Basically, as psychologists and researchers Ellyn Bader and Peter Pearson point out, "Couples lie to preserve their relationships, but it's those very lies that create dissent and leave the partners feeling stagnant, isolated, and alone."[1]

TYPES OF LIES

We can identify three basic types of lies. We already mentioned the "little white lies" we feel are harmless. Second, there are the lies of omission, the things we do that affect our spouses that we conveniently avoid mentioning. Third, there are the shameful lies we use to really protect ourselves and our image.

Little White Lies

A white lie is supposed to be a "good" lie, or a small insignificant lie. That's why we give it the modifier *white*. These are the lies we all justify. They are supposed to cause no harm to anyone. When we are caught in a little white lie, we often say, "What's the big deal? No harm, no foul!" But what we often forget is that what is little to us, may not be little to the other person.

An example of a little white lie could be the husband who is going to the doctor the next day for what could be a serious medical problem. When his wife offers to go with him he says, "No, that's not necessary. I can handle it." He would love for his wife to go with him, but he doesn't want to inconvenience her, nor does he want to appear to be vulnerable and needy. So what he says covers up his true feelings. It also shuts out his wife and deprives her of the opportunity to support him, and to know that the medical report she gets from him is complete and accurate, saving her stress and worry.

The other example of little white lies is the excuses we make for someone else. When the husband doesn't want to visit the in-laws, his wife will make some excuse for him. She'll talk about how busy he is or mention the business conflict he had—all little white lies to protect the feelings of the spurned in-laws.

White lies are usually motivated by our own needs rather than by the needs of the person we somehow think we are protecting. And they are often ineffective. Usually we may know we're being lied to, but we agree that it's no big deal, so we let it pass. But sometimes it hits a nerve, and the person challenges the little white lie. When it's found out to be a lie, the feeling of betrayal is very real. This is true even when we told the little white lie because we felt a friend or boss couldn't handle the truth, or wouldn't want to hear the truth.

Lies of Omission

Lies of omission are built on the principle that what we don't know can't hurt us. A husband spends money a couple doesn't have on something he knows his wife wouldn't approve of, and he doesn't tell. If he's found out, his excuse is, "Oh, I forgot to tell you." Or a wife buys an outfit that costs more than it should. She puts it in the closet and "forgets" to tell her husband.

Sometimes it's a bigger issue, as when the husband keeps silent about the financial crisis the couple is in and how close they are to bankruptcy. His silence is meant to protect her, but obviously it is also to protect himself from being seen as a failure in his wife's eyes. Of course if we were to sit down with him and discuss the futility of his efforts to keep this secret, he would agree. But he just can't bring himself to share the bad news. He knows that he is living a lie—a lie of omission—and even knows it's going to catch up with him.

Often when we lie by omission, we become obsessed with what we want to say to clear up the truth, but it seems like we can never find the right time to say it. As you obsess in your mind about what you left out, you begin to notice that you are feeling more distant from your spouse. You feel alone even when you are together, and long silences that never bothered you before become uncomfortable.

Another form of lie of omission is when we tell only part of the truth, or when we shade the truth so that it's not quite the truth anymore. The husband who visits a strip club with his clients tells his wife only that they went out for dinner. He leaves out where they went, or if asked, he lies and says they went somewhere else. Now his lying has moved into the third type of lie—the shameful lie.

"Shameful" Lies

If the wife of the husband who is hiding their financial crisis confronts her husband about their situation, he might be tempted to tell a "shameful" lie: a lie designed to cover up his shame. The husband who is caught in an affair through a photograph will attempt to cover his shame by saying "That's not me," even though everyone who looks at the photograph knows it is him.

Shameful lies are designed to protect us from the disgrace the truth would bring. And even when it is futile to lie, we do so as an attempt to cover up our humiliation. The husband who entertained his clients at the strip club, if caught, might protest to his wife that he had no choice—that's where the client wanted to go, or that's where the boss wanted to take the clients, or any other number of additional lies on top of lies to cover the shame of what he did.

The more shameful our behavior, whether it is something we did toward ourselves or toward our spouses, the more likely we will try to lie our way out of our shame. Of course we are then left with the shame of our lies, so the situation spirals further and further down.

Most of us hate to be lied to, yet we still lie. When we are on the receiving end of the lie, we somehow feel we are being manipulated and patronized in ways that basically disrespect us and our personal autonomy. And any lie when found out will either erode or destroy our trust in the other person.

CONSEQUENCES OF LYING

The issue of truth is an issue of trust. The basic foundation of any marriage is trust. In the beginning of a marriage, there is a blanket of trust that envelops a couple. Over time the little lies begin to chip away at trust. We may not even recognize the subtle distance growing between us as our trust is being eroded little by little.

For example a wife has lied to her husband for years about her actual age. She is five years older than him, and years ago told him she was a year younger. Over the years she was always careful not to let her actual age slip. But now she is approaching Social Security time and she's more worried than ever. She wonders if she should skip her benefits for six years, or should she finally tell her husband the truth? If she tells him the truth, will he wonder what other secrets she has withheld from him over the years?

While her husband is ignorant of the issue she is struggling with, her lie years ago probably has distanced her from him in ways she may not even recognize. Now the possibility of facing the truth pulls her away as she worries about what to do. If her husband asks, "What's wrong?" she can't tell him, or she tells him a lie about something else. At some level trust is affected and the level of intimacy in their marriage is harmed.

In the movie *The Cactus Flower,* Goldie Hawn's character says that a man who lies cannot love. If true it would be equally true of the woman who lies—she cannot love either. I'm not sure if the original statement is totally accurate, but I think it is clear that someone who is lying in any way to his or her spouse is not working at closeness and intimacy in the marriage. The lie may work for a time, but ultimately it will lead to distrust and distance in the relationship. So let's look at the secret of a great marriage.

Tell the Truth

Couples in great marriages have learned how to be truthful and open with each other. They can communicate with candor. They not only know how to speak the truth in love, they know how to hear the truth in love. As a result they rarely, if ever, lie to each other. Truth gives the couple a foundation of trust and mutual respect. They know their relationship is strong enough to handle any circumstance when it is dealt with openly and honestly.

TRUTH IS A TWO-WAY STREET

The apostle Paul gives us the foundation for this secret. Openness and candor are key components in our building a great marriage. The underlying principle is found in Ephesians 4:15, where Paul says we are to "speak the truth in love." This principle is also the foundation for what he teaches a little later on in the chapter. He says we are to "put off falsehood and speak truthfully to [your] neighbor [including your spouse], for we are all members of one body" (verse 25 NIV). The New Testament passage references a verse from Zechariah, where the Old Testament prophet tells the people, "These are the things you are to do: Speak the truth to each other" (8:16 NIV).

For Paul, telling the truth is a part of our new nature as God's adopted children. In his letter to the Colossians, he writes the same thing in the form of a warning: "Don't lie to each other, for you have stripped off your old sinful nature and all its wicked deeds" (3:9 NLT). Here he tells us that lying is a part of our old sinful nature. As new creations in Jesus Christ, we are to strip off those old patterns. In this context, we are to stop lying!

Hearing as Well as Speaking

What we need to see is that telling the truth is a two-way street. It is one thing to be able to "speak the truth in love," and it is another thing to hear the truth in love. When a wife responds to her husband's question about his weight, she needs to be truthful and loving as she says, "Yes, your weight bothers me." But he also needs to be loving in his acceptance of her truthful statement and not become defensive.

Even though the husband has asked the question, he needs to be certain he wants to hear the answer. And if he doesn't like the answer, he must in some way resist the automatic defensive response. The test in your being able to speak the truth in love has so much to do with how your spouse responds back to you. If he or she becomes defensive, you are not on the two-way street of speaking and listening—you both just slip into wanting to protect yourselves. So the spouse asking for a truthful answer must have a strategy for how to avoid the tendency to become defensive. We have to really desire to hear the truth. We'll look at some strategies for hearing truth in the next chapter.

TRUST—THE FOUNDATIONAL ISSUE

Just as there are two sides to "speaking the truth in love," there are two sides to the issue of trust. One side involves being able to trust someone else—entrusting ourselves to them. The other side involves being trustworthy ourselves. Now this creates a predicament, for no human is completely trustworthy because we are all sinful human beings. But being in a pattern of telling lies makes for a shaky foundation. We all know we will mess up from time to time, but we do not want to live a lifestyle that avoids telling the truth. A great marriage seeks to build trust with a commitment to honest, loving communication.

Entrusting

We said earlier that marriage typically begins with a blanket of trust covering both spouses. We try to pick someone as a spouse who is going to be worthy of our trust. We do this for the simple reason that there are a lot of untrustworthy people out there, and we want to be married to someone who isn't going to use us for a personal purpose. If you always have to be on guard with your spouse, you will be forced to live defensively, and that separates you emotionally from the one you marry. A healthy marriage requires that you be able to trust your spouse.

But sometimes our own ability to trust others has been marred, either in our growing up years and/or in the earlier years of our marriage. It is extremely difficult for us to take off our protective gear and be vulnerable. Trust makes us vulnerable to the one who can disappoint us or let us down. So we struggle with letting down our guards and becoming vulnerable because we have been hurt so many times before. The person who hurt us even claimed to love us, therefore we find we cannot entrust ourselves to any one person.

People who cannot entrust themselves to any one person find ways to trust a little part of themselves to one person, a different little part of themselves to another person, and another little part of themselves to a spouse. The end result is that all of those relationships end up feeling hollow and empty, while we fool ourselves into thinking that at least we are safe from the great pain we might experience by being vulnerable.

Being Trustworthy

The other side of the trust coin is being trustworthy, or being able to be trusted by your spouse. When we believe we are being trusted, it feels good. Our self-esteem grows as we feel our character is being validated. When we experience being trusted in a work situation, we work harder because we feel valued. And when we feel trusted in our marriages, we are on the path to a great marriage. It is an essential ingredient for a truly intimate marriage.

A key part of our being seen as someone to be trusted is the way we handle the truth. Intimate trust calls us to be completely honest. We place the interest of our spouses above our own when it comes to truth.

Openness

Openness does not mean we volunteer everything we are thinking. It doesn't mean we say things out of the blue like, "Your hair looks awful today" or "That dress makes you look fat" or "You look like a slob" or "I hate your parents." Even though we may think these things at times, they are not examples of openness. Openness goes deeper than merely articulating all of your free-associated thoughts. What it does mean is that a husband or wife reveals things to a spouse that the other *needs* to know for his or her own good, or it means things he or she *wants* to know about that are going on both in the other person's individual life and in their shared life as a couple.

If the bank calls today about an overdraft, you don't hide that from your spouse. That kind of information fits either the "need to know" or the "want to know." If you had a bad review at the office and your job is on the line, that certainly fits the "need to know" category. Obviously the two-way street of trust operates on the same level as the two-way street of speaking and listening in love. When one spouse reveals what the other needs to know, the hearing spouse needs to listen with trust and understanding that they are in the marriage together.

If you have an active foundation of trust in your marriage and you are placing the interests of your spouse above your own, one person doesn't just go ahead and act on what he or she wants when you disagree on some basic issue. You trust each other enough that you don't act until you have worked through everything surrounding the issue. The trusting environment of a marriage requires you to go beyond your own self-interest and to invest the time and energy to hear and understand your spouse.

Respect and Pride

Trust and respect go hand in hand. You show respect for your spouse by valuing his or her ideas and opinions. But understanding how respect works gives us more insight into how trust works in a marriage. For example if a husband truly respects his wife and she doesn't agree with something he wants to do, as a part of respect he is going to listen to and hear her thoughts on the matter. He is going to value and take seriously what she is saying, and she is going to feel valued. He is going to slow down the process, choosing not to act unless and until they can come to a satisfactory agreement on what to do. The same process goes the other way as well, when the wife wants to do something and there is disagreement. She listens to him and does not act until there is agreement.

Another aspect of being trustworthy in marriage is genuinely taking pride in what your spouse is doing, who he or she is, caring about and supporting his or her efforts. You show you are trustworthy when you can set aside your own self-interest and show real satisfaction in your spouse's accomplishments, being there when he or she is being honored by others.

CONCLUSION

Family therapist Frank Pittman writes, "It takes very little misinformation to disorient and destroy a relationship. I often point out to people that if I gave them detailed instruction on how to go from Atlanta to New York City, and I threw in only one left turn that was a lie, they would end up in Oklahoma."[2] That's what happens when we leave out one little detail that would change a whole story.

No matter how we rationalize a lie and no matter what type of lie it is, a lie is always the enemy in marriage, capable of destroying intimacy. Lies, secrets, and betrayals destroy trust. And trust that has been built over a lifetime can be destroyed in a moment. On the other hand, the good news is that trust can be rebuilt. But it will take time, energy, and consistency to put trust back together again.

In the next chapter, we'll look at how trust can be rebuilt.

1 Ellyn Bader and Peter T. Pearson, *Tell Me No Lies* (New York: St. Martins Griffin), 2.

2 Frank Pittman, *Private Lies: Infidelity and the Betrayal of Intimacy* (New York: W.W. Norton & Company, 1990)

CHAPTER ELEVEN

Humpty Dumpty Had A Great Fall

Whh en Humpty Dumpty had his fall, all the king's horses and all the king's men couldn't put him back together again. When one spouse lies to the other, trust in the marriage lies splintered, just like Humpty Dumpty. Fortunately when we break trust in a marriage relationship, unlike Humpty Dumpty we can be put back together again. But first we need to go back to the time before we fell off the wall.

WHEN WE TELL THE TRUTH

A big part of how we handle hearing the truth begins with the way the truth is spoken. Speaking the truth in love often means that you soften how you begin the conversation, and it also involves asking questions in a way that doesn't put your spouse on the spot or back him or her into a corner. To do this you need to be aware of the preconceived conclusions that you bring to the discussion.

Step 1: Soften the Way We Begin

Joe and Amy were victims of Joe's effort at being truthful. The day before their appointment, Joe confronted Amy about what he perceived as her failure to follow through on a counseling assignment we had given them the previous week. Amy's immediate response was to become defensive, and now as they sat in my (Dave's) office, Amy wasn't speaking.

I suggested to Joe that he ask Amy what he had asked her the day before but to soften how he asked the question. He tried but failed, as Amy responded in anger saying, "You're still blaming me, and I'm fed up with you doing that!" I pointed out to Joe that his "softer" wasn't really very soft.

"What were you trying to find out from Amy?" I asked.

"I really just wanted to know how she felt about the assignment. I didn't think I was blaming her for anything."

"Why don't you slow down your inquiry and simply ask her how she felt about the assignment" I suggested.

He did, and even though she was sitting there listening to my coaching, she responded to his softer approach to his question. Then I sat there and watched a most wonderful conversation take place as she first shared with him how she felt about the assignment. Joe then responded by sharing how he was anxious about whether or not she did the assignment and how scared he was about their marriage. And then Amy responded with more of her feelings and some reassurance to him about where they were in their marriage, and then they hugged each other!

After sitting there in silence for a minute or two enjoying the moment with them, I asked Joe if he could see the difference in the three ways he asked the question. He did.

"I can see now that I put her on the spot yesterday as I jumped to a conclusion that she didn't care about doing the assignment," he explained. "Then when you asked me to soften my question, I simply asked her if she cared about the assignment, and I can now see that I was still putting her on the spot. When I simply asked her how she felt about the assignment, that gave her room to respond—and I loved her response!"

The first step toward reducing a tendency to become defensive is in how we approach a conversation that could be confrontational. We need to soften how we ask our questions and do so in a way that leaves a lot of room for response.

Take a moment and talk together about a recent misunderstanding. Discuss ways that the beginning of the argument could have been softened. Discuss also how questions could have been more open-ended so as to allow more room for the other person to respond.

Step 2: Accept Each Other's Imperfections

It also helps to remind ourselves that neither we nor our spouses are perfect, and we are not going to do and say things perfectly. If we can consciously understand this, it can help us give the other grace in a situation where we might otherwise put up walls and get defensive.

Giving grace instead of becoming defensive means you operate on the assumption that your partner is not out to get you or to hurt you (we're talking here about early in the discussion or argument) and that the other has your best interest at heart.

How different many hurtful discussions would have been if we had only said at the beginning, "Somehow I'm feeling attacked right now, and I don't think that's what you mean to do." Once again this means that we slow things down, we don't jump to a negative conclusion, and we clearly and lovingly comment on what we are experiencing. If you or your spouse have a tendency to speak too quickly or out of anger, learning this new response will take some self-control. The Holy Spirit can help you with this discipline as you prayerfully ask to grow in this area.

Take a minute and talk together about an argument you had where you initially misread your spouse's motivation. Discuss statements you could make in the future that could slow things down in order to better understand the message as it was meant to be delivered.

Step 3: Listen to Your Own Anxiety

Jerry had been trained as a kid to be defensive about almost anything said to him. He grew up in an atmosphere of constant criticism from both his mother and father. His pattern continued into his marriage, and Pam, his wife, said, "I can't say anything to him without him becoming defensive." Here's a simplification of what he had to do in order to break the pattern and learn to listen with love.

First, he had to take the time to listen to what was going on inside of him. If Pam said something to him that in even the slightest way felt like criticism, he was transported back to the anxiety of his growing up years. As he and Pam discussed how she could talk to him without him perceiving criticism, Jerry first had to calm the anxious feelings that immediately asserted themselves inside of him.

As he talked with Pam about those early anxious experiences, she was let in to a part of Jerry that he had never really talked about. She knew how critical his parents were, for she had experienced their criticism herself firsthand over the years. But Pam had never heard Jerry talk about how it had affected him as a child living at home and as a young man. Prior to this, Jerry had said, "What's the point of talking about it? It happened, it still happens, and there's nothing I can do about it." What he didn't realize was that as he talked about this with Pam and she empathized with him over his anxiety, her understanding of what he had experienced changed him. He found that he was less and less likely to respond to Pam as if she were one of his parents. Talking about these early experiences with the one you love, who listens empathically, does create change.

When you stop and listen to yourself while you are being defensive, what anxieties are being stirred up within? Take some time to talk together about how this occurs in each of you, as what is really going on inside is typically unrelated to the spouse. Prior relationships with family play a big part in how we hear our spouses.

Step 4: Work on Not Personalizing What Is Being Said

Obviously this is easier said than done, but it is possible. Some of us have a natural tendency to personalize things, and we have to work even harder at this step. One of the best ways to do this is to realize what you are doing.

This usually means that you stop talking about the subject under discussion and talk instead about the struggle you are having internally by personalizing what is being said. The speaker can defuse the issue by starting the conversation with something like this: "I know you tend to personalize, and I don't mean for you to hear this in a way that is an attack on you, but I need you to hear what I'm saying." Sometimes when we predict how the other person is going to respond, we minimize his or her tendency to respond that way.

Discuss together how each of you tend to personalize things. If one or both of you do this, talk about how you can better start conversations to help the other not take the issue at hand too personally. A couple needs to try to understand that the issue being raised is not just about them, but it's about the marriage. Moving outside of yourself is an important part of communication.

Step 5: Be Supportive in Your Response to Your Spouse
Remember that the reason we are looking at these steps is so we can better "speak the truth in love" to each other, as well as "hear the truth in love." The more you can assume that your spouse is working on the "in love" part of both of these tasks, the more you can be supportive. And the more supportive you can be, the greater your experience of intimacy with each other will be. And that's your goal. The "in love" element of both of those statements means in part that you are always thinking of how your words are going to affect your spouse. If you really want to show your spouse you care, be open and honest, even about the little things. And when you are on the receiving side, show your love by assuming the best of motives and that you are both working toward the same goal— a deeper, more loving marriage.

WHEN WE DON'T TELL THE TRUTH

Trust is something that is definitely earned. When a couple is trying to recover from some breach of trust, such as an extramarital affair, it is hard to regain what is lost. Over the years whenever a couple has come to counseling because an affair has occurred, the injured spouse almost always says something like this: "I've always said that if he (or she) ever had an affair, I was walking away. I would be done with the marriage. But now that it has happened, I really don't want to give up on my marriage."

In that statement he or she is quietly asking, "Can broken trust ever be repaired?"

An affair is one of the biggest lies a spouse can bring to a marriage. In fact an affair is built on lies, and the longer the affair goes on, the more the lies multiply. But there are other lies that break trust.

Secrets are lies. A husband who has a secret bank account is lying to his wife every day that account is open and active. We've talked with husbands and wives who have had secret mailboxes where they receive the bills for their secret credit cards. What a husband or wife does on a business trip that is unspoken is a secret and therefore a lie. So is leaving out an important detail regarding a situation that a spouse should know about. What he or she doesn't know *does* hurt the marriage and will eventually destroy trust.

Have you ever noticed that when we lie to our spouses, we usually have a good rationalization for the lie? We may be thinking that they can't handle the truth, that the lie could threaten the marriage, or some other self-deception. Even the rationalization is a lie—it's a lie we tell ourselves. Regardless of what the issue is, a spouse usually recognizes rationalizing when it is going on and can almost feel the trust eroding. When we don't tell the whole truth, we may be able to prevent an argument, but there are consequences to this choice.

Can Trust Be Repaired?

We always answer this question in the affirmative. Yes, it can, and that's the important work of any relationship. Because we are all sinful, dysfunctional people who at some time will prove ourselves to be untrustworthy, every important relationship in our lives will require the rebuilding of some trust at some point in time. Sometimes it may be only a slight remodeling, while at other times it will be a complete rebuilding process.

In some of our relationships, it may seem much easier to just cut and run. We decide the relationship isn't worth the effort of rebuilding. And this may be true in some situations, but seldom is it ever true of marriage. You might even say that one of the purposes of marriage is to teach us how to rebuild trust when it is broken. Here are the steps to take when trust needs to be rebuilt, directed primarily at the person who has betrayed trust.

Step 1: Offer a Sincere Confession of the Truth

Let's use an affair as an example. Regardless of how the spouse finds out, healing begins when the betrayer confesses the whole truth. Let us be clear on this point: The whole truth does not mean every intimate detail. That puts too much of a burden on the shoulders of the betrayed spouse. The rule of thumb concerning how much to confess is this: If I want to seriously rebuild trust with my spouse, I confess anything that would undermine the rebuilding of trust if it were to be found out later.

Sometimes the betrayed spouse wants to know every detail. Our counseling experience has clearly shown that knowing every detail isn't going to help the healing process. It will only mean the couple has more to deal with, and it will lengthen the healing process. One woman we know spent four years digging for every detail of her husband's affair. She interviewed the other woman twice. She was looking for an answer to "Why did he do this?" She lived through four years of torture and delayed the healing process for herself and her marriage. There is no satisfying answer to the question "Why?"

If you are dealing with a less painful betrayal, the principle is still the same. If information has been withheld in the form of a secret, or if one spouse has been lied to about anything, the need for a sincere confession of the truth always marks the starting point. Without it rebuilding cannot move forward. Couples who try to sweep any kind of lie under the carpet risk lessening or even losing the intimacy they long for.

Step 2: Practice Complete Openness

This is an essential part of the healing process. The spouse who has had an affair has given up control of his or her life at least for as long as it takes to rebuild trust. He or she must give up control by becoming an open book to the other spouse. No secrets allowed. Cell phone bills, travel itineraries, whereabouts at any given point in time, complete accessibility—all of these are part of becoming open to your spouse about all aspects of your life. Anything less than complete openness restricts the rebuilding of trust.

What does a wife do with a husband who has a secret mailbox and secret credit card? The question is really more: What is the husband willing to do to regain her trust? He has to find ways to show her that he has no more secrets. Showing her his credit report after several months have passed would help. Discussing with her every penny he makes and where it goes would help.

Again the principle is one of complete openness. There can be nothing that remains hidden, or else when it is found out—and it will be—it will destroy the trust that was reestablished. And when trust is breached a second time, it is more serious. The old adage says, "Fool me once, shame on you; fool me twice, shame on me." Few marriages can survive a "fool me twice."

Step 3: Exhibit Genuine Sorrow

This is also a key to rebuilding trust. Without genuine sorrow it is like building a brick wall without cement. It simply won't hold!

We've watched the reaction on a wife's face when her husband has said, "That's it. I've told you I'm sorry, and if that doesn't help you, too bad. It's over; just get over it!" That attitude leaves the issue of trust completely broken. We've had other husbands say to us, "How can I let her know how sorry I am?" And our advice is always, "You tell her 'I'm sorry' as sincerely as you know how, and you keep telling her until she's sick of hearing it."

The goal of rebuilding trust is that at some point there is genuine sorrow on the part of the one who lived the lie and genuine forgiveness on the part of the one betrayed. Without both of these conditions the marital reconciliation is going to be very superficial and unsatisfying to both parties.

The principle is the same, even for the little lie of omission or the little white lie: When confronted by my spouse, or when I take the initiative to start the process, I need to confess the truth, become completely open about the subject, and show genuine sorrow for my betrayal. Every lie in a marriage is a form of betrayal, and so regardless of the seriousness of the betrayal, the process is the same.

Step 4: Realize That Rebuilding Trust Takes Time and Patience

The rebuilding of trust always takes time. The more serious the offense, the more time it will take for trust to be repaired. A small lie of omission may take a couple of days, whereas an affair may take a year or two just to get to level ground again. So rebuilding means both the offender and the offended need to be patient with the process.

SOME OTHER TRUST ISSUES

Let's look at some other ways truth and trust can be an issue in a marriage. Let's imagine that Tom sees his married friend with a group of men going into a strip bar. Does Tom tell his wife, Sue, what he saw? What if he tells her, and she gets suspicious about how he knows this? Or what if he tells her, and she shares it with all the women in her Bible study group? How does Tom decide what is the right thing to do?

Or let's imagine that Mary is at one of the mailbox stores, and as she walks in she sees her friend Sarah pulling some mail out of one of the mailboxes. Sarah acts very defensive and finally says, "I would appreciate it if you would keep this as 'our little secret.'" Does she confront Sarah at another time and place? How does Mary decide what to do? Does Mary tell her husband, Andy? What if Andy is Sarah's husband's boss? How does that affect her decision?

Tom's and Mary's situations are different, but they both pose threats in both of their marriages. What does Tom tell his wife, and what does Mary tell her husband? Truth and trust are at stake here. The basic issue of trust in their marriages weighs in the balance. And the question becomes how much does Tom trust his wife with this information, and how much does Mary trust her husband with this information?

Then, of course, if there are trust issues for either Tom or Mary, they risk compounding those issues by some rationalized lies of omission. At some point we may all be faced with this kind of situation. And the questions at stake here are how much do Tom or Mary really trust his or her spouse, and how open with their spouses are they willing to be?

Take some time to discuss Tom's and Mary's situations. How would you answer the questions raised? If either Tom or Mary had concerns about their spouse's responses, what safeguards could they have taken?

Based on what we've discussed in this chapter, although there may be a downside to either Tom or Mary sharing information with a spouse, if they are going to build their own great marriages, then truth has to be the guideline. If their marriages are their top priorities (as we will learn about in the next chapter), there can be no question about them sharing with their spouses what they saw and what their concerns are.

Great marriages are built on what Jesus said: "You will know the truth, and the truth will set you free" (John 8:32). In our marriages the truth will set us free to become all that God wants us to be, together as a couple.

Who's Number One?

CHAPTER TWELVE

*"We'd have a great marriage if
I felt more important to my husband. All he cares
about are his work and his friends."*

We both love college football. We love autumn, and football represents the welcome arrival of the fall season. We have our favorite teams, and we love it when they win. One thing we get a special kick out of is when, midway through the season, a team that so far has struggled is close to winning its first game. As the TV camera pans the crowd, ecstatic fans are cheering the team as they count down the final seconds to victory. We see the fans raising their index fingers in the air as they shout, "We're No. 1!" In the polls their team wouldn't even be in the top 25, but in the hearts of the fans, it's right there on top.

If feeling like you are No. 1 is important in football, you can imagine how much more important it is in marriage.

Before we look at how being No. 1 in the eyes of our spouses affects our marriages, we need to be clear that in this chapter we are talking about human priorities. It is a given that God is to be the top priority in our lives. We aren't questioning that basic principle. It is the underlying theme of everything in this chapter. Our concern here is not how God fits into our priorities, but how our priority lists stack up in reference to the relationships in our lives.

MARRIED TO THE MINISTRY

In the early years of our marriage, I (Dave) worked as a leader for a youth ministry. Before starting I went through an intensive two-week training program. The trainers were all men who were legendary in this particular ministry. It was a privilege to have them spend time working with us. Near the end of the two weeks, I remember one of the leaders saying, "Men, you're now married to the ministry! This is your priority."

I took that statement very seriously, especially considering its source, and I determined that maxim would launch me into an important new level of commitment to ministry. It certainly seemed like that principle was a part of the leader's success, so I took it to heart. I can remember driving home to be reunited with Jan with that thought echoing in my head. My guess is that every man there who heard that statement took it as earnestly to heart as I did.

But I'm not sure how many of them were naïve enough to arrive home and announce to their wives, "Honey, I'm now married to the ministry." Yes, that's what I actually did! If others did they probably received the same response I did. A strange look came over Jan's face, and she said, "Hmmm, I thought you were married to me." I don't remember my response, but it didn't change my attitude. It took a number of years for me to get it right and undo the damage I had done to our marriage by accepting and living out a wrong priority.

When I made my announcement, in so many words I was telling Jan to move over because she was being replaced by my new love. Ministering was now No. 1. Obviously Jan wasn't pleased with my new commitment. Looking back I can see that this led to a lot of struggle and pain in the early years of our marriage, and that struggle continued until I got the priority thing right. The priority scheme that placed ministry as No. 1 wasn't the way God designed us to live.

Fortunately for our marriage, I had a pastor friend and mentor who about five years later sat me down on a weekly basis over several months and showed me from Scripture that after God, my wife was to be my earthly priority, followed by my family, and *then* followed by my ministry. And if I got that order mixed up, my ministry would suffer. "That," he said, "was really God's plan."

Seldom in the church today will you hear such a direct statement like the one I heard during my training. Saying it out loud may have been a product of that time period. But there are still many men and women in ministry who believe their ministries are to be the top priority in their lives, even before their spouses and their families. You can probably achieve a "good-enough" marriage this way, as long as both spouses agree on those priorities. Some couples have grown comfortable with a marriage that does not hold top priority. But our goal should be higher than a good-enough marriage. Furthermore we believe there is a price to pay for such choices: The relationship will suffer. And that isn't God's choice for what is best for you and your spouse.

Stable Marriages With Mixed-Up Priorities

We have encountered a number of marriages that have failed because one spouse had his or her priorities all wrong. Mixed-up priorities don't build marriages. But over the years we have also encountered a number of stable marriages that weren't marriage-centered. We've met couples who were very ministry-centered. That's all they did and all they talked about. Their kids were involved as well. The marriages were stable because both spouses were ministry-centered and accepted the fact that their marriage wasn't as important to them as their ministry.

We've also met couples who were very career-centered or work-centered. And they too had reasonably stable marriages. If fact most of our society's middle class probably would go under if couples weren't work-centered.

Think of the days of the Great Depression. We've talked with couples who described their parents—in particular their fathers—working two jobs for years just to hold the family together and help the kids get ahead.

While Dad worked two jobs during the week, and sometimes a third part-time job on the weekend, Mom worked hard at keeping the home and kids on track. These couples were convinced that if you would have asked their parents about their marriage, they would have said, "It's good! We make it happen." Perhaps they would feel the marriage was good because they were in survival mode, and it was good just to be able to survive.

We have also seen some stable marriages that follow their cultural patterns by making their parents their top priority. I (Dave) remember asking one husband when he would become an adult in his culture. He understood that by my question I was asking him when he would be free from making his parents a priority. He answered, "When I die." He could tell by the puzzled look on my face that I didn't understand. "Even after my parents die, I am supposed to honor them as if they were still alive. It's only when I die that I get that kind of honor on my own."

We've seen other stable marriages in which the individuals were both very self-centered. They had built an independent kind of relationship where the marriage had a lower priority than other areas of their lives. Many of them had reached a level of financial freedom that allowed each to have whatever he or she wanted, and they indulged themselves.

Probably the most common type of marriage that we've encountered is the child-centered marriage, in which everything revolves around the children. It's clear that for them the kids are No. 1. That even includes marriages in which the kids are grown, married, and on their own, and they still are the top priority for the parents. For these couples the kids will always be No. 1.

Each of these nonmarriage-centered marriages succeed in the way they do because both spouses put the same thing ahead of the marriage on their priority lists. What they don't realize is that they are also putting a lot of unnecessary pressure on their marriage relationship, and they are limiting the quality of the marriage they experience.

An Ancient Example of Shifting Priorities

This isn't only a contemporary problem. When you turn to Genesis in the Old Testament, you encounter several marriages that were very child-centered. Look particularly at the account of Isaac and Rebekah in the book of Genesis, chapters 24 to 28.

When we first meet Rebekah, she is a beautiful young woman who immediately catches the eye of Isaac's father's servant. Abraham had sent this servant to find a suitable wife for Isaac after Sarah, Isaac's mother, had died. When the servant met Rebekah, he knew this was the right woman for Isaac, and after some bargaining and sharing of family news, Rebekah agreed to leave her family and return with the servant to marry Isaac.

As the servant and Rebekah were returning to Isaac and Abraham's home, Isaac was taking a walk out in the fields, meditating. He saw the servant coming at about the same time Rebekah sees him. She asked the servant, "Who is that man walking through the fields to meet us?" And when told it was Isaac, Rebekah covered her face with a veil and went to meet Isaac. After the servant explained everything to his master, "Isaac brought Rebekah into his mother Sarah's tent, and she became his wife. He loved her deeply, and she was a special comfort to him after the death of his mother." We can picture their relationship like this:

Isaac   **Rebekah**

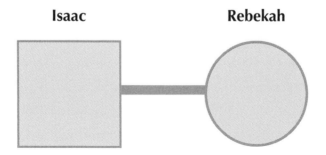

At first we see here a wonderful marriage-centered relationship. Isaac and Rebekah represent a beautiful love story. At the beginning of their marriage, there was a strong love attachment between these two people. We already noted in the verse quoted previously that Isaac loved Rebekah very much. They cared deeply about each other. But then the kids came along—twins. Everything changed. And for Rebekah it started when the twins were still in the womb. These two boys started competing with each other even before they were born. One of the most critical times in a marriage is at the birth of the first child. How the couple responds to the addition of a new life to their marriage sets the direction for the marriage in the years ahead. And Isaac and Rebekah did not respond well to the addition of children to their marriage.

For one thing Rebekah came from a very manipulative family. We not only see this in her; we see it in her brother Laban when we meet him later in the story. One thing manipulative people like to know is who has the power. When they know this, they are better able to manipulate the people and the situations. Following Rebekah's asking God what was going on between these two brothers in her womb, God told her that some day the younger one would rule over the older one—he would be the one with the power.

And then when the babies were born, Esau, the oldest, turned out to be a strange-looking baby. He was covered all over with red hair, sort of a "wolf man junior." And Jacob was a beautiful baby. Remember, Rebekah had kept it in her heart that the younger one would be the powerful one, and when she saw how beautiful the younger one was her heart became attached to Jacob. Her relationship with Jacob would eventually become more important to her than her relationship with her husband, Isaac. And Isaac was left to fill in the gap by caring for Esau. Over time these coalitions between Rebekah and Jacob and between Isaac and Esau, became more pronounced. Jacob was a real mama's boy, while Esau got leftovers from his dad. And Isaac and Rebekah gave very little, if anything, to each other. We can diagram their family and its coalitions like this:

Isaac   **Rebekah**

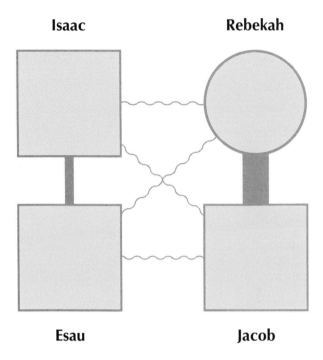

Esau   **Jacob**

The primary relationship in this family as the boys grew was between Mom and Jacob. The relationship between Isaac and Esau was really secondary. Rebekah poured all of her emotional energy into Jacob, neglecting her relationship with Isaac and with Esau. What started out as a beautiful marriage-centered love story turned into a child-centered marriage. Eventually it led to emotional distance and estrangement between Isaac and Rebekah.

This estrangement comes to a head in Genesis 27, when Rebekah sets up Jacob to lie and deceive his father so he can steal the blessing from his brother. In this episode it becomes clear that Rebekah's loyalties were to Jacob, not to her husband.

The beautiful love story over time turned into a bad marriage relationship. This is often the result of any marriage that is not marriage-centered. That is why it is important to not settle for what we think is "good-enough." God's model for marriage is always better than our own conventional wisdom. He desires us to place our spouses above any other earthly priorities for a reason—to protect what is sacred. And we know that what often starts out as good at some point becomes empty and can even turn bad. Avoiding that path leads us to the next secret shared by couples in great marriages.

SECRET NO. 6:

Put the Marriage First

Couples in great marriages live out the belief that the primary relationship in their lives, humanly speaking, is their marriage relationship. Their marriage supersedes all other human relationships to the point that both spouses have made the other spouse their priority, and each spouse knows that.

MARRIAGE AS THE PRIMARY HUMAN RELATIONSHIP

This secret is based on the importance the Bible places on marriage. In the Creation story in the first and second chapters of Genesis, two unique things are established. One is the principle of the Sabbath rest—that one day in seven is to be different. That principle was and is a part of Creation. The other is marriage. Marriage is also a unique part of Creation. By their placement in Creation, God made both of these—the Sabbath and marriage—of prime importance.

Look at the importance God gave here to marriage. God said, "It is not good for the man to be alone. I will make a helper who is just right for him" (Genesis 2:18). But before he did, God brought all the animals before Adam so he could name them. And in doing so Adam realized that there was no one like him. As Adam realized his aloneness, God caused him to fall asleep, and then he made a woman from the man and "brought her to the man" (verse 22). Here is God the Father bringing his daughter Eve to her future husband, just as countless fathers have done with their daughters as they have given them away in marriage. Adam was excited because here was his counterpart, his companion, his bride. And by the end of the chapter, Adam and Eve were husband and wife.

The first marriage took place in the Garden of Eden—the marriage relationship is that important! No other human relationship is as important in God's plan as the marriage relationship, for no other relationship is presented as part of Creation. In addition Proverbs 18:22 says that "The man who finds a wife finds a treasure, / and he receives favor from the Lord."

So what does this mean for us? If we go back to the situation in Isaac and Rebekah's family, we can illustrate what this means in each of our families.

MODERN-DAY ISAAC AND REBEKAH

Let's imagine that Isaac and Rebekah are our contemporaries and that Esau is a problem child. In Genesis Esau likes to hunt and fish, so let's imagine that his contemporary problem is that he is always skipping school to go fishing, and he is hanging around with the wrong kind of friends. Isaac and Rebekah turn to you for help. You could spend a lot of time trying to help Esau get his priorities in his life right. Friends and other family members could show him how important school is to his future and to his future earning capabilities. He might agree with everyone about this, but when he goes home to his highly dysfunctional family, he will probably say to himself, "What's the use? I'd rather go fishing than go to school."

The problem doesn't change because his behavior is basically a protest against what has been going on in his family for as long as he can remember. His constant sentiment of "What's the use?" is really related to the feelings of rejection he has experienced as he has watched his mom clearly favor Jacob over him. He has also felt his father's powerlessness as he has watched their marriage deteriorate over the years as Rebekah has poured all of her energy into Jacob. At some level he is protesting the coalition that exists between Rebekah and Jacob that shuts him out of a relationship with his mother.

So how do you get Esau's attention? You do it by working on the primary relationship, the one that lays the foundation for all of the other relationships in the family: his parents' marriage. The way the family is now working is that each son has one parent on his side. But this sets it up so there is also one parent who is not on each son's side. When problems arise that son can work the parent on his side to be against the other parent—he can become a wedge between Mom and Dad, diverting attention away from himself and getting his parents to disagree about him. Eventually the wedge becomes so severe that the marriage suffers. Mom and Dad don't work as a team anymore. They are at odds with each other. When Mom gets upset because Esau won't go to school, Dad says things like, "So why is school so important? It didn't help me. Leave him alone." And they are at each other once again.

If, however, we view the marriage as the primary relationship in the family, then we can create change in this family by strengthening the primary marriage bond so that Isaac and Rebekah work together as a team again. They support each other on issues, even when they don't fully agree. They stand together and do not let either of their sons drive a wedge between them. Rebekah has to become more supportive of Isaac than she is of Jacob. And Isaac has to become more supportive of Rebekah than he is of Esau. If we can heal the marriage, we can heal the family problems. That's the power of seeing the marriage relationship as the primary human relationship.

PUTTING THE MARRIAGE FIRST

Ron and Kim are a modern day example of this principle. They came to counseling because their 16-year-old daughter had run away from home several times. The last time she ran away she put her life in danger.

During the early meetings another counselor and I (Dave) worked together with the whole family. We started by asking Sally, the 16-year-old daughter, and Sam, the 12-year-old son, a lot of questions about how they viewed their family. Who was close to whom? Who did the discipline? How did their parents get along? And so forth. Eventually we saw a clear pattern emerge, and at the beginning of the third session, we turned to Sally and congratulated her on her loyalty to her family. Mom and Dad thought my colleague and I were the crazy ones at that point, but then we quickly pointed out to the parents that we believed Sally had become a family problem in order to keep her mom and dad together.

We went on to say that we believed they were close to getting a divorce, and the only thing that was stopping them was the problem they were having with Sally. And therefore we wanted to work with them on their marriage. We dismissed the kids from counseling, and the other counselor worked with Ron and Kim on their marriage. We found out that Ron was indeed ready to leave the family until Sally had run away.

Once the parents were in counseling, Sally never ran away again. Fixing the parents' marriage fixed the running-away problem. That's the power of keeping the marriage relationship the top priority. When the marriage is the priority, the rest of the family is secure. Someone has said that loving one's spouse is the best gift a parent can give a child. That's because it makes the marriage relationship primary.

OTHER CULTURAL PATTERNS

Most cultures do not view the marriage as the primary relationship. Over time these cultures have redefined the primary relationship pattern away from the marriage.

If we look at family structure in a typical Asian family, the primary relationship is between the mother and the oldest son. She is often closer to that son than she is to her husband, and that mother-son relationship is what is valued in the culture. In most Middle Eastern cultures the primary relationship is between the father and the oldest son. We knew a student from Nigeria who said that in his culture the primary familial relationship was brother to brother.

When someone says to us that making marriage the primary relationship is really a Western cultural value, we are quick to point out that we think it is really the biblical pattern. These other cultures have effectively turned away from the biblical pattern, and it is clear in our own culture right now that there are strong efforts to turn us away from the primacy of the marital relationship. Whenever this has happened in other cultures, those cultures have become less of what God designed humankind to be. We have to make efforts to expose cultural lies and promote the belief that God's standard is what is best.

CONCLUSION

Often parents worry about shortchanging their kids if they take the time to keep their marriage relationship a priority. It's helpful to remember that parents only have to be "good enough." In fact the closer we get to "perfection" as parents, the more damage we do to our kids. "Perfect" parents—parents who never limit or frustrate their children—produce children who grow up to believe they are entitled to anything they want. Even as children they become little monsters, ruling the family to their own detriment.

When a couple makes the decision that they are going to be the best parents they can be but that their priority is to continually work on their marriage relationship, they teach their children an important lesson— that marriage is the primary relationship in God's plan for us. And if parents have a strong, loving marriage, their kids will not only feel more secure, they will also have a model for the kind of marriage they want to have when they become adults.

CHAPTER THIRTEEN

Making Time For The Marriage

During the middle years of our marriage, we went through a difficult time with one of our kids. It was a trying time on every member of our family and put incredible stress on us as a couple. We attribute our successful navigating of those years to two things.

One, we prayed together as a couple every day. There were some days when we were so stressed we didn't even know what to pray and our prayer was simply "Lord, help us!"

Two, every Friday morning during those difficult years we headed to a beachfront restaurant for breakfast. For years neither of us scheduled anything else on Friday mornings. The workweek ended late on Thursday night; Friday morning was our time together. We would arrive at the restaurant when it opened at 8 a.m. and many times we would stay until almost lunchtime. Our only agenda was to be together for those two or three hours. Our appointment together was a sacred commitment! God used it to strengthen our relationship in so many powerful ways through the years.

Some Friday mornings we would just sit and let the ocean breeze bring healing to our souls. Other times we would deal with some problem we faced, or we would plan our calendar for the next weeks, or we would resolve some unsettled issue between us. We did whatever we felt like we needed to do to stay connected to each other.

FIFTEEN MINUTES A DAY

We've told many couples about the impact those Friday mornings had on our marriage. We've suggested that they find some time when they can get away from the kids and all the problems of the home and just check in together as a couple.

Many couples have responded by saying they have a hard time identifying a time they could set aside on a weekly basis. So now we suggest that they set aside just 15 minutes a day to simply sit together and talk about their days. Many couples decide to spend an additional 15 minutes at the table after dinner is finished. They tell the kids to go and play, and they'll call them when it is time for them to do their kitchen chores. An extra cup of coffee together adds to the ambience as they simply share with each other the events of their days. Nothing heavy or earth shattering—just connecting with, "How was your day?"

We've had couples who were on the verge of divorce make the small commitment to the 15-minute-a-day drill. One couple found that the quarter hour easily became an hour or two as they finally became interested in each other's lives. The divorce they were contemplating disappeared as a topic of discussion as they rebuilt a loving relationship together.

Take some time now to discuss together what kind of weekly or daily commitment you will make simply to be together in a nonpressured situation. Do you want to commit to a weekly breakfast or lunch? Or does catching up with one another for 15 minutes after dinner fit your schedule best? Whichever way you decide to spend focused time together, remember it is a commitment—you cannot cancel it unless you both agree and set a replacement time. Your commitment to these together times communicates to your spouse that she or he is your priority.

YOUR PRIORITY LIST

Take time to think about your priority list as it stands right now in your life. We've listened to a husband defend himself as his wife tells him she doesn't feel like she is very high on his priority list. "You think my priority is my work," he protests, "but I only work this hard to provide the lifestyle you like." She responds by saying, "Oh no you don't. You love your work more than you love me." This is dangerous ground, but if you want to move your marriage to great, you need to take the risk and talk together not only about your priorities but about how your spouse perceives your priorities. Take some time now and seriously think through the priorities in your life. Then list below the top five priorities you have—as you see them.

Exercise 1

The Husband's List:

1. _____

_____

_____

2. _____

_____

_____

3. _____

_____

_____

4. _____

_____

_____

5. _____

_____

_____

The Wife's List:

1. _____

   _____

   _____

2. _____

   _____

   _____

3. _____

   _____

   _____

4. _____

   _____

   _____

5. _____

   _____

   _____

Once you have each written out your list, set a time to discuss each one. A warning in advance: How you order your priorities will probably be different from your spouse's list. Even the items on the list will be different. That's to be expected. Take turns explaining why you feel each item belongs where you have placed it on your list. Then listen as your spouse explains a different perception of priorities. Sometimes items and priorities are different because a spouse has already taken care of a concern or an issue.

A LOOK AT YOUR NEEDS

Your priority list sometimes has a lot to do with how well your needs are being met by your spouse. And your needs are often closely connected to unspoken expectations. When you examine your expectations, notice how often they are unexpressed. The result is that your needs are often quite different from what your spouse perceives them to be. And that misunderstanding directly relates to additional feelings that your needs are not being met. Until you talk about your priorities, you can feel like you are walking in circles, often traveling to places you didn't want to go in your relationship.

Take the time for each of you to respond to each of the other's statements and then discuss why you responded the way you did. Discuss what behaviors both of you might adopt to bring your expectations closer in alignment with your spouse's expectations for marriage.

Exercise 2

1. When it comes to my needs in our marriage, I think:

    a. my needs are greater than yours.

    b. your needs are greater than mine.

    c. our needs are about the same.

2. I think you depend too much on getting your needs met:

    a. from outside sources.

    b. from sources inside our marriage and family.

3. The way this affects our marriage is _____.

4. It would help if:

    a. we could express our needs more openly.

    b. we didn't talk so much about our needs.

    c. or _____.

Often the unstated expectations of your spouse cause you to blame him or her for your emotional reactions. And because you cannot read the other's mind, you need to find ways to talk about these expectations. Taking advantage of an open moment instead of using your scheduled "together time" is often more productive.

It's the Little Things

We were traveling together, and Jan had time to do a quick load of laundry. When she was done, I was surprised to see that she had washed some of my things. I hadn't expected her to do this and didn't need my clothes to be washed, but it felt good that she had done it for me. We talked about it and noted that it is often the little thoughtful things we do for each other that make us feel like we are our spouse's priority.

It reminds us of a popular song entitled "Little Things Mean a Lot." Here are the lyrics:

Blow me a kiss from across the room,
Say I look nice when I'm not.
Touch my hair as you pass my chair,
Little things mean a lot.

Give me your arm as we cross the street,
Call me at six on the dot.
A line a day when you're far away,
Little things mean a lot.

Don't have to buy me diamonds or pearls,
Champagne, sables, and such.
I never cared much for diamonds and pearls,
'Cause honestly, honey, they just cost money.

Give me your hand when I've lost the way,

Give me your shoulder to cry on.

Whether the day is bright or gray,

Give me your heart to rely on.

Send me the warmth of a secret smile,

To show me you haven't forgot.

For now and forever, that's always and ever,

Little things mean a lot.[1]

We counted 10 little things just in these lyrics that a spouse can do to show love and caring. We've talked with couples who were convinced that they could never do enough to make their spouses feel like they were important to them. We love to point out that it takes a lot less time than you think, but it does take some attention to detail. See if you can identify the 10 caring things listed in the song and then talk together about some of the other little things your spouse can do for you that communicate that you are important to him or her. List here some of the little things you each do for the other.

_____

_____

_____

_____

_____

_____

_____

_____

SOME PRIORITY PRINCIPLES

Here are some important principles to keep in mind as you work together
on making your spouse feel like he or she is No. 1 with you:

- **Recognize that your attitude—not your words—communicates your
priorities.** You can say over and over that your spouse is your top
priority, but if your attitudes and actions don't back up the words,
the words are empty and meaningless. It is a proven principle that
when your attitude and actions contradict your words, the other
person will believe your attitude and actions and ignore the words.

- **Work hard at protecting the marriage.** If your spouse is your No. 1
priority, you will do everything possible to protect the marriage and
protect your spouse. (Isaac and Rebekah didn't protect their
marriage. They became overly involved with their children.) Your
children are important, but never as important as your marriage.
Long after your children are grown and gone, we trust you will still
have your marriage. You need to protect it along the way.

- **Show that you enjoy being married to your spouse.** This is an
extremely important attitude to communicate. We remember a
young man who had recently married who said to us with
enthusiasm, "I am so happy being married! I never imagined it
could be so special." His wife could pick up on that attitude and
knew she was his No. 1.

- **Care about the little things and be willing to sacrifice your own
needs to keep doing the little things.** It's the accumulation of little
things over time that gives us assurance of being loved. And even
when you know you put your spouse first, you should keep on doing
the little meaningful things for him or her.

As you discuss these points, remember that what really matters is perception. When you understand that your spouse's perception of any given situation is reality for him or her, you will add some strong building blocks toward having a great marriage. When we can get a couple to give up the search for placing blame—who is right and who is wrong—and see that each person's perceptions represent what is true for them, they are each suddenly free to hear each other. That is a powerful motivator for a great marriage.

1 Edith Zinderman and Carl Stutz, "Little Things Mean A Lot."

All's Fair In Love And War

"We'd have a great marriage if only my wife would quit pressuring me to do more than my share."

"All's fair in love and war." The saying is familiar, and most people probably focus on the idea that in romance and battle anything goes. We are zeroing in on the other element: what's fair. In this chapter we want to consider the subject of fairness in marriage.

Many marriages have foundered over the fairness issue. "I'm doing more than you're doing, and that's not fair!" Or like the case of the husband quoted on the previous page, some marriages founder because one or both spouses are just too greedy. They have expansive expectations of their spouses while at the same time they seem to have minimal expectations for themselves.

Larry and Renee argued constantly about the unfairness they perceived they were experiencing in reference to each other. They set up elaborate guidelines so that everything was "fair." When it came to money, each spouse had his or her own income and checking account. Early in the marriage, Larry calculated the ratio between their incomes, and they came up with a rough calculation of how the bills could be divided along that same ratio. Each New Year's Day, Larry sat down and recalculated both the income and the total of the bills so he could update the ratios and make a fair division of expenses.

It didn't stop with their money. Larry had a regular meeting every Tuesday evening, which left Renee home alone with the kids. So to keep things fair, Renee scheduled every Wednesday evening for whatever she chose to do. Sometimes she went out with friends, other times she stayed in her room and read. Her time started at the same time Larry left for his meeting and ended at the same time Larry typically returned home. After all, it had to be fair.

Responsibilities like putting the kids to bed, transporting the kids to various activities, and anything else Larry and Renee were called upon to do as parents were carefully divided to keep things evenhanded. Larry and Renee's expectations weren't really greedy in that they didn't expect too much from each other. They just expected that everything in their marriage had to be in perfect balance.

THE PROBLEM WITH FAIR

But fair isn't what it's advertised to be. There are at least three problems that develop when a couple becomes obsessed with everything needing to be balanced, even, tit-for-tat.

First, whether a couple knows it or not, the need to be fair requires that scores be kept. *Keeping score is the antithesis of love.* In the Bible's famous chapter on love (1 Corinthians 13), the apostle Paul writes that true love "keeps no record of being wronged." If you're keeping score in your marriage, you are counting not just all the good things you're doing but also all the wrong things—or lack of things—that your spouse is or isn't doing.

Because keeping score is the antithesis of love, it also works counter to trust. The only reason you as an individual keep score is to make certain that everything is fair. And that sort of belief system says that if you don't keep score, things will quickly become unfair. So keeping score gives your spouse the subtle message that "I don't really trust you to be responsible and participate in the marriage." Trust really means you don't have to keep score.

Second, whenever you focus on things being 50/50 in a marriage, you are building a marriage on a *foundation of fear.* If you don't trust your spouse to be fair, you can become fearful that in some way your spouse is going to use or abuse you. Both of you are afraid that one or the other or both is not going to do their fair share. What if you only do 49 percent? How will your spouse respond? What if you get sick—how will you make up what you have failed to do? Whenever trust is absent, fear moves in and takes over.

Third, you set yourself and your spouse up to build *silent resentments*. If you perceive rightly or even wrongly that you are doing 51 percent, you are setting the groundwork for resentment. And often it is a silent resentment because you're not really certain about that 51 percent. If you complain, your spouse may prove to you that he or she is the one who is really doing the 51 percent, or even 52 percent.

If the fear that comes from not trusting a spouse doesn't become detrimental to the marriage, then the silent resentment building up in you can end up being the very thing that destroys the marriage.

We don't often see how trying to create our own mechanical system of justice in marriage can be destructive because there can be a pleasurable side to bitterness and resentment. The wise King Solomon wrote in the book of Proverbs that "Each heart knows its own bitterness—and no one else can fully share its joy" (Proverbs 14:10). We've always been struck by the way King Solomon placed bitterness and joy together, but it's really the same thing as when we refer to someone having a "pity party."

Bitterness can be a subtle enemy, creating a strange kind of joy— the pity party. Then, as it gets a hold on us, it brings trouble. Look at the warning given by the writer of the book of Hebrews in 12:15: "Look after each other so that none of you fails to receive the grace of God. Watch out that no poisonous root of bitterness grows up to trouble you." It is interesting to note that not only does the bitterness destroy a person, but many others are also destroyed by its poison.

THE DANGER OF DISILLUSIONMENT

How does bitterness spread its poison? Perhaps the most common way is through an attitude of disillusionment. What happens is that as your bitterness grows silently within, you begin to look at your spouse and think that he or she is not the person you thought he or she was. Your resentment feeds into a sense of disillusionment, and at the same time, your disillusionment feeds into more resentment. Ultimately you come to a place where you think your spouse is not the person you want to be with because he or she no longer lives up to your expectations. You then find yourself considering leaving your spouse and desiring a replacement that will better meet your hidden expectations.

This spiral of disillusionment and resentment often seems to come to a head around midlife. We look at our spouses and families, and because of the silent resentments we have built up within, we can only see a dark future with these people. So like a business owner, we decide we need to fire everyone, close up shop, relocate, hire a new staff, and open a new office. Usually in time, if our resentments have grown out of a search for "fairness" or some other disappointments, we find that the new staff at the new shop is really no better than the old staff and that somehow we didn't get it right this time either.

One of the grand illusions that individuals fall prey to is the illusion that *I deserve to be happy* in my marriage. And the next thought is *My spouse is the one who must make me happy.* If he or she isn't meeting expectations, then there is a problem. Do I stay in the unhappy situation? is the question this line of thinking evokes. Unfortunately the bad thinking continues into believing the lie that a new person to love or a new location will change everything for the better.

Couples who break out of the score-keeping cycle or the "I deserve to be happy" fantasy find that it is like breaking free from a curse. They have lived under this spell either because that was the model they saw in their parents or it was some cultural expectation they believed. Instead of grandiose expectations of what their spouses are going to do for them, the spell is broken and they begin to work in the reality of what they can do for their spouses.

This unconditional kind of relationship is known as "agape," one of several Greek words for love. C. S. Lewis wrote, "Agape is all giving, not getting."[1] This is what couples in great marriages experience, and it is the basis for Secret No. 7 of how to have a great marriage.

SECRET NO. 7:

Focus on Giving, Not Receiving

Couples in great marriages have discovered that they quantify their contributions in terms of 75/75 or 100/100, not 50/50. Their focus is on giving, not receiving. They do not keep score but willingly give above and beyond what's expected—without resentment—knowing that there will be times when their spouse gives more.

MARRIAGE AS A COVENANT

This secret describes the fact that a couple has recognized. They have moved from the tit for tat of a contractual arrangement to the giving attitude of a covenant relationship. They have the distinction between a contractual relationship and a covenant relationship. Most of our culture views marriage as a contract between two people. A contractual relationship is built on the "as long as" each person lives up to the stated, and even unstated, expectations and terms of the contract. With a contractual relationship, we are in the relationship "as long as you perform as I expect" and "as long as I perform as you expect me to." If either fails to perform, the contract can be broken.

Think of some of the things couples say as they divorce that reflect a contractual relationship. "He wasn't the person I thought he was," or "I can't live with that kind of behavior," or "She crossed a line that I'm not willing to accept." Of course some of these statements may have some serious issues underneath, but think of them as conditional statements made about the marriage. That's the nature of a contractual marriage.

In contrast to the contractual marriage, a covenant marriage is built on "regardless of." It is an ongoing relationship that continues *regardless of* how well either spouse performs. In fact it isn't based on performance. It is based on the promise made and the vows exchanged. In his Pulitzer prizewinning drama *The Skin of Our Teeth,* Thornton Wilder has the main character, Mr. Antrobus, describe the nature of a covenant: "I didn't marry you because you were perfect. I didn't even marry you because I loved you. I married you because you gave me a promise. That promise made up for your faults. And the promise I gave you made up for mine. Two imperfect people got married and it was the promise that made the marriage. And when our children were growing up, it wasn't a house that protected them; and it wasn't our love that protected them—it was that promise."[2]

That promise forms the foundation of our covenant, of our marriage. And there are no conditions attached to that promise.

WHAT IS A COVENANT MARRIAGE?

Some states have created what they call a Covenant Marriage License.[3] In Arkansas, for example, when the law was passed, the governor and his wife took out a Covenant Marriage License and remarried to establish their marriage as a covenant. They did so to set an example of what they wanted couples in their state to do as well.

What covenant marriage means in most states is that a couple has to pass certain measurable requirements both before the marriage and after the marriage. For example, they are required to take a series of premarital classes at least six months prior to the wedding. Then after they are married, if the marriage gets into trouble, they commit to going to marital counseling and are required to commit to a cooling off period that delays by a substantial period of time their ability to divorce. If they divorce, both people must agree to the divorce—it isn't the typical no-fault divorce where only one person wants to divorce and the other is helpless to stop the divorce.

This practice doesn't exactly illustrate what God meant by the term "covenant," but it is a move in the right direction to attempt to build stronger marriages and to make people think twice before divorcing.

The idea of the covenant comes from the ancient Middle East. Covenants were agreements made between rulers, and often the only requirement was for a conquered party to swear loyalty to the conquering authorities. In exchange for their loyalty, the conquering party made certain covenants with their new vassals, such as protecting them against any other enemy.

These covenant relationships became the model for how God described his relationship to his people, the Israelites. He established a covenant with them through Noah, then renewed it through Abraham, and then renewed that covenant again through David. It is a commitment that God made to his people, and it stood firm even when the people disobeyed. That's why it was called an "everlasting covenant." The book of Hosea is a parable that illustrates the everlasting power of a covenant relationship. In God's covenant with his people, and in the marriage covenant, the covenant relationship is based on the principle of unconditional love.

One not familiar with the idea of covenant might ask what happens when there is a major offense, such as a betrayal of some kind that takes place in the marriage. What if one person becomes totally disloyal to the covenant and breaks faith?

An Ancient Tale of Commitment

The Old Testament prophet Hosea answers that question for us by using his own life experience as an example of God's commitment to his people in spite of their betrayals.

In his account Hosea represents God's unconditional love for Israel, and Gomer, Hosea's wife, represents the people of Israel who have been unfaithful in their loyalty to God. Hosea is asked to go and marry a prostitute and have children with her. He does this, and Gomer, his wife, gives birth to two sons and a daughter, each named to convey some prophetic message to the people. Then Gomer leaves Hosea and goes back to being a prostitute.

In chapter 2 of Hosea, which is an interlude between the story of Hosea and Gomer, God likens himself to Hosea. He says, "But now bring charges against Israel—your mother—for she is no longer my wife, and I am no longer her husband" (Hosea 2:2). But then a few verses later, God reverses himself and says, "I will fence her in with thornbushes. I will block her path with a wall to make her lose her way. When she runs after her lovers, she won't be able to catch them. Then she will think, 'I might as well return to my husband, for I was better off with him than I am now'" (Hosea 2:6-7). However, Gomer doesn't make the choice to return to Hosea, nor does Israel return to God.

Then God tells Hosea, "Go and love your wife again, even though even she commits adultery with another lover" (Hosea 3:1). Here is the powerful picture of the nature of a covenant. There are no conditions, just loving commitment. It is a relationship that is based on the "regardless of." Of course the obvious question is, How do you do that?

The Healing Power of Forgiveness

In Hosea's case he brings Gomer home, but they do not just pick up life and live as if nothing had happened. There is a period of time for healing. Hosea says to Gomer, "You must live in my house for many days and stop your prostitution. During this time, you will not have sexual relations with anyone, not even with me" (Hosea 3:3). There is a transition time of healing they must go through. And this healing takes place in the context of forgiveness. Forgiveness for a serious offense such as Gomer's takes time, so there was the work of forgiveness that was required in order to move ahead.

Forgiveness is the glue that holds a covenant marriage together. Therapist Gary Thomas says, "One of marriage's primary purposes is to teach us how to forgive."[4] Building a great marriage together requires an ongoing ability for both spouses to forgive each other for the many small irritating things that take place, but also a commitment to work through the forgiveness process for any major issues that occur.

Canceling the Debt

To forgive someone means that we cancel the debt they owe us.[5] Offenses in a marriage are a form of debt that the offender owes. For example when

I (Dave) don't treat Jan in the way that I should, I owe her something more than just an apology. Let's say I have made a commitment to her to meet her at some place at a specific time, and it is very important to her that I be there at that time to share in something that is only happening at that time. But I get caught up in something I'm doing and fail to make the appointment on time. By the time I get there, the reason she wanted me there is gone—it's too late.

All of my explanations and apologies do not change the fact that I failed to be there when I said I would. And I disappointed her. Because we can't reverse time, I can't fix the problem. I'm left owing her a debt that I cannot pay. Her disappointment cannot be undone by my doing what I failed to do. That's where forgiveness comes into the picture. If forgiveness is the canceling of a debt, then when Jan forgives me, she is canceling the debt that I owe her. She knows I can never repay the debt I owe her. Most of the forgiving we do cancels a debt that cannot be paid back.

Now multiply this over time with all of the things that I do that disappoint and hurt Jan and all of the things she does that hurt and disappoint me. Without the healing power of forgiveness, we have mutual unpayable debts, and they just keep growing. And if we let the debt pile up, we are also letting resentment and bitterness grow. And our love for each other gradually grows cold.

THE MYTHS OF FORGIVENESS

It's important to review some basic principles about some of the myths that many people believe about forgiveness.

First, forgiveness is not forgetting. True forgiveness never means we forget—in fact as humans we can't forget. The saying "forgive and forget" is an old myth that has been recorded as early as the 13th century. It is also a myth that can be found in almost every culture. But it is obviously not a statement of truth.

We often hear it expressed something like this: "I can't forget, so therefore I must not have forgiven." It can be very freeing to realize that forgiving and forgetting are not synonymous—in fact there is no relationship between forgiving and forgetting. Sometimes it can be dangerous to act like we forget by pretending the offense never happened. It can set us up for a repetition of the offense and added pain and hurt.

Second, forgiveness never condones the wrong that has been done. Some people believe that if you forgive someone, it is like saying that the wrong committed didn't matter—that to forgive is to act like it was nothing. But this simply isn't true. It is important to see that in most situations, forgiveness only benefits the forgiver, not the forgiven. The offender is not off the hook but is no longer a debtor (and may not even know this). Banks forgive loans they cannot collect. One doesn't need to understand accounting to know that banks do this for their own benefit— they don't like the "burden" of uncollectible debts in their financial statements. In the same way, the person extending forgiveness no longer carries the burden of the debt owed to them—they have cleared their account, so to speak. They are not owed anything anymore. And in canceling that debt, they have eliminated the possibility of developing bitterness and resentment.

In a marriage the one who benefits from forgiveness is the forgiver, but in a marriage our goal is for forgiveness to pave the way for reconciliation. However we need to keep forgiveness separate from reconciliation. It only takes one to forgive, but it always takes at least two for there to be reconciliation. The goal in marriage is always to work toward reconciliation, but that is where the role of the offender comes into play.

Reconciliation requires genuine forgiveness, but it also requires genuine sorrow on the part of the offender. If I (Dave) miss my important appointment with Jan and I don't really care that I have hurt her, she can still forgive me, but any reconciliation we have will be superficial; there probably won't be any reconciliation until I can show her I am truly sorry.

Being forgiven when you are the offender involves more than just being truly sorry. It also carries with it the obligation for you to acknowledge the offense and to take responsibility for what you have done. You are doing these things when you can understand and empathize with the pain you have caused. You willingly and genuinely affirm yuour guilt and your sorrow.

But forgiveness is not our natural response to being hurt. We would much rather seek revenge even though we know that revenge only sets up a cycle of repeated efforts at getting revenge. When God says, *I* will take revenge; *I* will pay them back" (Romans 12:19 NLT), he is directing us to participate in the unnatural response of forgiving.

So there is willfulness involved when we forgive, and it can't just be a superficial "You're forgiven." We have to move against our natural tendencies to either minimize the hurt, excuse the offender, or nurse our wounds in silence as resentment builds. In addition when Jesus commands us to "forgive your brothers or sisters from your heart" (Matthew 18:35 NRSV), he is saying that forgiveness is more than just the words. When we forgive we are acknowledging the offense and the break it has caused in our relationship, but we are also expressing a forgiveness that is genuinely heartfelt. To get our hearts in line with forgiving would imply that some offenses are going to take longer to forgive than others. We either need to be working toward forgiveness or be willing to forgive.

We've already talked earlier about the rebuilding of trust. Our genuine sorrow over the pain and hurt we have caused helps in the rebuilding of trust. So does taking the initiative to actually be the one who asks for forgiveness. This act is a part of our effort at rebuilding the trust that may have been broken or at least damaged.

FORGIVING OURSELVES

One of the most difficult tasks we often face is forgiving ourselves. To keep our marriages healthy and growing toward greatness, we cannot afford to have an attitude of unforgiveness toward ourselves. When we have been forgiven by God and when we have been forgiven by our spouses, it is quite arrogant to hold on to an attitude of unforgiveness toward ourselves. Holding that attitude sometimes gives us the false feeling that being unforgiving toward ourselves in some way protects us from repeating the offensive behavior. It also results in our living in a prison of self-imposed guilt that serves no useful purpose. And, instead of protecting us, our attempts to hold on to the feeling of not forgiving ourselves often sets us up to repeat the hurtful behavior.

We've found over the years that when people forgive themselves, they also from a form of self-imposed bondage. We are all imperfect people. We need to forgive each other for our imperfections, but at the same time, we need to forgive ourselves. Forgiving your spouse along with forgiving yourself frees you not only to be more truly yourself, but it leads to an openness in your marriage that does lead to greatness.

---

1 C. S. Lewis, *The Collected Letters of C. S. Lewis, 18 February, 1954*, W. H. Lewis, ed. (New York: Harcourt Brace Jovanovich, 1966), 256.

2 Thornton Wilder, *The Skin of Our Teeth* (Harper and Brothers, 1942).

3 For more information on marriage as covenant, visit www.covenantmarriage.com.

4 Gary Thomas, *Sacred Marriage* (Grand Rapids, MI: Zondervan, 2000), 167

5 For an expanded discussion of forgiveness, see David Stoop, *Forgiving the Unforgivable* (Ventura, CA: Regal Books, 2001).

CHAPTER FIFTEEN

Growing Beyond Fair

We spent some time in the previous chapter exposing how the pursuit of fairness can be extremely harmful in the covenant relationship of marriage. The drive for desiring complete fairness in the marriage is often the unspoken expectation we bring to the table. In chapter 13 we looked at some of our expectations that are connected to our needs. Before we are married, we talk about a lot of our expectations and work on developing important mutual goals. But all too often after we are married, we stop talking about these dreams and we stop talking about the new expectations we are developing in our hearts for our marriages in the future. We just don't think to take the time to discuss them with our spouses.

Here is a fun exercise that will not only help you articulate some of your more recent dreams for your marriage but will also help you set a course that will allow some of your dreams to come true. It is an exercise that will keep the dreams alive, and the idea is that you are imagining what your marriage will look like five years in the future.

Exercise 1

Imagine that it is five years in the future, and you run into a close friend that you haven't seen in some time. As you catch up with each other, your friend asks, "How are you doing in your marriage?" When you reply that "Wow, everything is just perfect. I can't believe how great my marriage is," your friend looks skeptical. So you begin to list for your friend everything that is happening in your relationship with your spouse that makes your marriage perfect for you.

Now you can assume anything. You can assume that any stressors in your life are all behind you. Any issues that have held you back in your marriage have been put to rest. After all it is five years in the future.

So write out on paper what you would tell your friend as you describe what makes your marriage relationship perfect for you. There is no wrong way to do this. You can put it in story form or you can make an outline. The format doesn't matter; just make a list of why your marriage relationship is now perfect for you.

You are to write out your list on your own, just as your spouse should write out his or her list on his or her own (you will end up with two separate lists). When you have both finished, set a time when you can sit down and read each other's lists. The only rule as you read each other's lists is that neither can criticize or make negative comments about what the other has written.

We have found over the years as we've asked countless couples to do this exercise that men and women often list similar things, but the order in which they list them is quite different. So the order in which you identify things doesn't matter—it does not communicate anything. This list is not prioritized.

Take the time to discuss the "what" and the "why" of your lists. It is important to remember not to become critical of each other's list. You can only respond positively to your spouse's list. Comment on anything in his or her list that surprises you or on anything that comes to your mind that you forgot to put on your list.

Once you have discussed each other's lists, choose something that you both agree should be a part of your marriage in the next five years, and then begin to discuss what you would have to begin doing now so that in five years this would become a reality. What would you be doing in three months? In six months? In a year? In three years? You are basically making this a goal-setting process, but at the same time you are working at finding ways to both express and to meet the growing expectations you each have.

WHEN LIFE'S NOT FAIR

Sometimes our struggle with fairness in our marriages mirrors what we watched in our parents' marriages, or what we struggled with in our relationships with either our parents or our siblings. Sometimes parents work so hard at being fair with their children that the quest for fairness becomes a way of life. The opposite is also true when parents weren't fair with us as children; we sometimes overreact in our adult relationships and seek to make sure that everything is fair.

Talk together about your experiences growing up that are related to fairness. Did you struggle with your siblings over what was or wasn't fair? Talking about these things together can help you understand why this may be an issue in your marriage.

Another aspect of fairness in our families of origin is the pattern of keeping score. Did you see your parents keeping score with each other? Did you do it silently in your own mind in reference to either your parents or your siblings?

Simply talking together about any of these patterns that may influence you in your marriage can be a powerful release. For one thing it helps our spouses better understand some of our internal issues. And when we can talk about this with our spouses, we are often exposing a family secret. This in itself is a powerful tool to break generational patterns that hold us back in our marriages.

IS YOUR MARRIAGE A COVENANT OR A CONTRACT?

A lot of what we struggle with in the whole idea of fairness is what a contractual marriage is built on. A contractual marriage is based on "If you do this, then I will do this. And if you don't do this, there will be consequences." You can easily see that a contractual form of marriage is concerned with keeping score and with fairness, as we've discussed earlier in the book.

A covenant marriage is quite different and is clearly about unconditional love. The Covenant Marriage Movement describes what couples who are creating a covenant marriage affirm:

> Believing that marriage is a covenant intended by God to be a lifelong fruitful relationship between a man and a woman, we vow to God, each other, our family, and our community to remain steadfast in unconditional love, reconciliation, and sexual purity while purposefully growing in our covenant marriage relationship.[1]

CHARACTERISTICS OF A COVENANT MARRIAGE

There are five components noted here that describe a covenant marriage:

1. There is a conscious recognition that vows are being made to God, to each other, to our families, and to our communities.
2. The couple will be steadfast in unconditional love.
3. The husband and wife will steadfastly seek to reconcile when there are problems.
4. The husband and wife will maintain sexual purity.
5. The husband and wife will purposefully continue to grow as a couple.

Two things pop out as I read this list of characteristics of a covenant marriage that are uniquely stated here. One is the use of the words "unconditional love." The other is to vow to purposefully continue to grow as a couple. While these may be assumptions in the minds of all couples who marry, they are intentionally noted here as being a part of the vows.

Take some time now to discuss together the difference between love, perhaps as it was defined earlier in the book, and unconditional love. What are some of the ways you have shown each other unconditional love? When is it difficult to show each other unconditional love?

How about the phrase that "we will purposefully continue to grow as a couple"? What are some things you can do to ensure that you will continue to grow together? What are some things your church could do to help couples continue to grow together in their marriages?

TAKING ACTION

Here are some things you can do to encourage the growth of covenant marriage principles in your church and community even if your state doesn't offer a covenant marriage license:

- Contact the Covenant Marriage Movement at www. covenantmarriage.com. They provide free information for your church or faith community.
- Create enrichment opportunities for couples. Some churches and some organizations put on marriage seminars and marriage retreats. Find out where they are being offered in your area and get some other couples to attend with you.
- Don't be afraid to get counseling when you get stuck in your own marriage. But make certain that the counselor you will be seeing specializes in working with couples together, not separately. Ask the counselor how he or she feels about divorce. All too many couples counselors are not pro=marriage and will not work as hard as you need to keep your marriage moving forward.
- Find an older couple you believe has a great marriage and ask them to spend time with you and your spouse to talk about what they have learned about marital success.

A RECOMMITMENT

You might also want to recommit yourselves to each other using vows that refer specifically to the covenant you are making with each other and with God. Here's an example: "Today I affirm this covenant with you, (spouse's first name), to live with you in accordance with God's will for our marriage and to reflect our covenant relationship with Him. I will love you, comfort you, honor and keep you, in sickness and in health. I will forsake all others and remain faithful to you so long as we both shall live, to the glory of God."

A HEAVENLY MODEL

One indication of the importance God places on our marriages is the fact that the apostle Paul uses marriage as a picture of our relationship with God. Paul quotes from Genesis and then makes a powerful affirmation about marriage. He says, "As the Scriptures say, 'A man leaves his father and mother and is joined to his wife, and the two are united into one.' This is a great mystery, but it is an illustration of the way Christ and the church are one" (Ephesians 5:31-32).

The oneness of marriage is really a "great mystery." And then Paul finishes this passage with the profound insight into how a marriage can work. He says, "So again I say, each man must love his wife as he loves himself, and the wife must respect her husband" (verse 33). When the man loves his wife as much or more than he loves himself and the wife shows respect to her husband, you have the basic ingredients for a great marriage.

Unconditional love and respect need to be felt by both partners. Talk together about how you as a husband show your wife that you unconditionally love her and respect her and how you as a wife show that you truly respect your husband and unconditionally love him.

THE WAY OF FORGIVENESS

How up-to-date are you in your forgiving? Forgiveness is the heart and
soul of a great marriage. Couples who have great marriages stay current on
their forgiving of each other. They give grace to their spouses. There are
consequences, of course, but relationally, grace and forgiveness pave the
path they walk together.

Exercise 2

Let's take some time to do an exercise that can catch us up on our
forgiving. You will each need a sheet of paper and an envelope.

Individually take the time to reflect on the regrets you have had over
the years in your marriage. They may have been dealt with or they may not
have been. Write down on the sheet of paper anything that comes to your
mind that has or might have affected your marriage relationship, whether
it has been forgiven or not. Don't write it out in detail; simply put some
key words down that represent what you are referring to. When you have
finished, fold the sheet, put it in an envelope, and seal it.

Exchange the sealed envelopes. Don't open them. Sit down across
from each other and hold the other person's envelope. Then in turn say to
your spouse, "Please forgive me for my failings in our marriage." Your
spouse responds, "I forgive you, you are forgiven." Then you in turn
respond, "Thank you. I now forgive myself."

When you have finished, take the envelopes and a large cooking pot.
Set fire to the envelopes and drop them into the cooking pot to burn to ash.
Don't watch the envelopes burn as you might see something that was
written on the sheet. Instead watch the smoke rise into the air and think of it
as the incense of forgiveness rising up to heaven itself. When finished take
time to pray together and thank God for the healing power of forgiveness.

We have done a similar exercise when we teach forgiveness in different parts of the world with a ministry called Youth with a Mission (YWAM). It is a powerful exercise, especially when each person watches the smoke rise from the cooking pot. When I've seen participants who have completed this exercise several years later, many of them have commented on how that experience had literally changed their lives and their relationships with their families.

IF I WERE TO DIE

In the first chapter of the book, we quoted Carl Whitaker saying, "As much as I would miss my wife if she were to die, I would miss what we are together even more. Our 'we-ness,' our 'us-ness.'" No one knows when they will die, so let's assume we need to prepare for the unexpected today.

Exercise 3

Take some time as you finish this book to write your spouse a letter. In this letter say all the things that you would wish you had said to your spouse if he or she were to die today. Here are some sentence starters that you can use in your letter:

What I would miss about us is _____

_____

_____.

What I've loved best about our relationship is _____

_____

_____.

What I wish we could still do together is _____

_____

_____

My biggest disappointment would be _____

_____

_____.

And you can add anything else to the letter that you would wish you had said. Take some time as you write your letter. You may need to do it in more than one sitting.

Then set a time and place to read each other's letters. You may want to go to your favorite restaurant or to a favorite spot that has meaning to you. Perhaps you can make plans to do something you have always wanted to do together. Make this a special and memorable occasion. Reading your letters, however, can be an emotional time, so you may want to save that part of your outing for somewhere more private than a restaurant.

Exchange your letters and read what your spouse has written. Take your time and let it all sink in. Then talk about your positive reactions to each other's letters. When you have finished your discussion of the letters, find a special way to end your time together. Take a walk or just sit close together as you pray.

Over the years we have found that there are those special times that you look back on. They are more than just memories, they are markers along the way that are part of the special history you have shared over the years you've been together. These three exercises have the potential to be special markers on your journey to greatness as a couple.

1 www.covenantmarriage.com.

CHAPTER SIXTEEN

Keeping Love Alive

Someone once said that every relationship we have is either growing and moving forward, or it is sliding backward and beginning to deteriorate. Relationships never stand still for very long.

We've certainly noticed that in our relationship. There were times when we not only were sliding backwards, we almost slipped over the precipice. But something always seemed to hold us, and eventually we would get back on track. Sometimes the movement forward wasn't easy or pain free. In fact in some of the darkest times in our family, we pulled together and not only grew as individuals but also grew closer as a couple. We're living proof that great marriages don't just happen; they always are the result of hard work. And as we look back, the results made the work worth it all.

FORWARD MOTION

In this chapter we want to look at some of the ways we can keep our great marriages moving forward. We want to look at three basic principles that kept us on track, and that we have shared with other couples with the same results.

PRINCIPLE NO. 1: WE'RE HERE FOR THE LONG HAUL

When we see marriage as a covenant as opposed to a contract, it is a given that we are here for the long haul—"until death parts us." Jack and Judith Balswicks, professors of psychology at Fuller Theological Seminary, point out that "the core characteristic of a covenant marriage is commitment, a factor that is profoundly important to marital stability, according to research findings."[1]

If you stop and read your wedding vows again, their very nature implies a covenant, not a contract. But few brides and grooms really think in terms of a covenant. As we said in an earlier chapter, the common attitude today is to see marriage as a contract, where the couple, while vowing for better or for worse and until death, operates on the principle that we are together as long as we each meet our end of the bargain. That's an attitude that feeds into the "short haul."

When Jan and I look back on the early years of our marriage, we stated earlier that we refer to this period as our "Great Tribulation." Our first ten years were terrible years together. Yes, we had some good times, but overall we did not have a good marriage. But we never considered divorce as an option. It wasn't a part of our vocabulary, consciously or subconsciously. We were both quite young when we married, and in many ways looking back on those years, we were struggling to grow up individually at the same time we were trying to grow together. But one thing was clear—we were determined to make it work.

We didn't think in terms of a covenant during those days, but we lived out the principles of a covenant. Looking back now we both realize that we understood our vows and we were there for the long haul for better or for worse. How different our lives would have been if we had given up because we were miserable. We eventually grew past our misery and started to build something special together.

Sticking It Out

A number of studies contain interviews of couples on the verge of divorce who of course report themselves as being miserable in their marriages. In many of these studies, the researchers go back and reinterview these same couples some years later. Invariably those who divorced are still unhappy, while most of those who stayed together report they are now happy. They had stuck it out through the dark winter season and found that the spring and summer really did come. That was our experience.

We've worked with couples who were miserable with each other but came to counseling because divorce just wasn't an option. We recently had a couple like that come back in to deal with some extended family issues. We hadn't seen them in years. Our last memory of them was them telling us they felt they had turned the corner in their marriage and now had the tools to get their marriage on a good track. Until they returned we had not known whether or not they had been successful. They spent most of the first session telling us about all the great things they had done together and how blessed they were in their marriage. They thanked us for helping them turn things around. What had been miserable—a cause for divorce for many other couples—was long past, and now they were in the process of becoming everything they had hoped to be as a couple.

Marriages do go through seasons as well as stages. When a couple can genuinely make an unconditional commitment to stay the course with each other in the cold, dark season of a marriage, not only does spring come, but summer as well. There is a saying that warns us not to doubt in the darkness what we know to be true in the light. You can take this and apply it to the seasons of a marriage. Don't question the vows and commitments made to each other in the light of the summer days when you have hit the dark of winter together. Stay the course. Love unconditionally. And know that spring will come.

PRINCIPLE NO. 2:
FOCUS ON WHAT IS THERE, NOT ON WHAT IS MISSING

When a couple is about ready to give up on their marriage, they often say that there is nothing positive going on anymore in the marriage. It's all bad. But John Gottman's research[2] found that not to be true. He found that in a healthy, growing marriage, positive behaviors outnumber negative behaviors by a ratio of at least five positives for every negative. For example this means that whenever I do a negative behavior that affects Jan, I must do at least five good behaviors to offset my negative behavior.

What happens as a couple's marriage begins to unravel is that the number of positives compared to the negatives begins to drop below the five to one ratio. Even in the good marriage, you can see that the negative behaviors have more power to impact us. But as the positive behaviors decrease or the negative behaviors increase, the negatives take on even more power because they are no longer being offset by the positive behaviors.

Here's the interesting point. By the time the couple is ready to divorce, the positive behaviors are about equal to the number of negative behaviors. The positives are not absent, except in the minds of the divorcing couple. And they aren't even outnumbered; they are just overpowered by the negatives.

Blinded by the Negative

In other words negative behaviors have a way of blocking our vision of positive behaviors. And this feeds right into the human tendency to focus on the negatives. Think about what happens when the boss says to you in the morning, "I need to talk to you later today. Come see me at 4:00." It is the rare human being that looks forward to a positive meeting with the boss under these circumstances. What we typically do is stew all day, worrying about what we must have done wrong to cause the boss to want to meet with us. It is our natural tendency to assume the negative, even when the negative isn't there.

Even the optimist can get caught up in seeing the glass as half empty when it comes to our behaviors in our marriages. It's like we take the positive behaviors for granted but can't let go of the negatives very easily. We are looking at what isn't there. But to keep love alive, we need to work at looking at what is positively there, not at what is missing.

If you did the caring days exercise, you had the opportunity to focus on positive, affirming behaviors. This is a habit that great marriage couples have developed—seeing the positives. They don't deny the negative behaviors, they just choose not to give them power to determine the state of the marriage. This isn't just a plug for optimism—it is a call to shift away from the natural human tendency to focus on the negatives.

Doreen and Jerry were caught in this negative cycle caused by their natural human tendencies. They had slowly grown apart after the kids had grown and moved out. They each had their own world. Jerry was caught up in work, and Doreen had restarted her career and was having a great time with new friends. They didn't talk much because their pattern while the kids were home was to talk about the kids. Now that they were alone, they typically had very little to say, even about the kids.

Over the two years they had been in the empty nest phase of marriage, they had also become very critical of each other. However, they seldom would articulate their criticism to each other, instead choosing to complain to their respective close friends. Finally they decided there wasn't much left of their marriage and it was time for them to go their separate ways. But Doreen convinced Jerry that they at least owed it to their kids to go to counseling.

It didn't take long in the first session for each to verbalize the critical images of each other that they had created in their own minds. They were hesitant at first, but then the negative complaints started to spill out into the open. We didn't let them go too far, stopping them and asking if they had ever said any of these things to each other before. Jerry kind of mumbled a "no" and then went on to describe how he had never told Doreen how he really felt, sharing it only with Bill, his best friend.

We asked them both the same question. "What has kept you together over these years?" You could almost feel the tension leave the room as they relaxed and started talking about their kids. It was obvious they had had a child-centered marriage and over time had grown apart silently. Now that the kids were gone, they felt their separateness.

After they had finished talking about their kids, we asked them how they met. Now they acted a bit embarrassed as they each offered to let the other speak first. Finally Doreen described the beginnings of their relationship, smiling as she talked. Then Jerry added some detail that Doreen had left out. They both became more animated as they talked about the early years of their courtship.

Then we asked Jerry what had attracted him to Doreen—what made her interesting to him? He thought for a moment and then described in great detail how he saw Doreen back then. When he finished we asked Doreen the same question—why had he been attractive to her? They had a fun time talking and listening to what each other said in response to our questions.

As they finished we asked them both, "How were you able to hide these attributes from each other after the wedding?" It was a loaded question—we knew they had just stopped noticing those things. They were caught up in looking at what they felt was missing and ignoring the very things that had brought them together at the beginning. When we can get a couple to remember the good things they saw in each other in the beginning of their relationship, the good feelings they recall about their spouse often last beyond that session and make our working with the couple easier in that subtle change of atmosphere. What we get them to do is look again at what is there, as opposed to only looking at what is missing.

PRINCIPLE NO. 3:
GIVE GRACE TO EACH OTHER

We've seen couples who supposedly still love each other but who almost invariably attribute some negative motivation to what their spouses are doing or saying to them. It is almost an automatic response, and it usually follows a pattern that was set in motion in childhood where in order to protect him or herself, he or she had to prepare for the worst and even assume the worst from a parent. Often when this protective pattern is carried over into the marriage, there is no rational reason for assuming the worst—it is just learned behavior.

Very little can put a bigger damper on the feelings of love than being misunderstood by your spouse in terms of your motivation for either what you are doing or saying. And at the same time, there is very little that is more powerful in keeping love alive than showing grace and forgiveness to your spouse.

The Balswicks say that, "Gracing love is a major component of the mystery [of marriage]. As agents of grace, each spouse participates in reciprocal interaction of talking and listening, giving and receiving, honoring differences and affirming giftedness, forgiving and being forgiven. The far-reaching effects of gracing love culminate in a deeply satisfying relationship."[3] In the same way a mutually gracing love thinks the best of the spouse's motivations and intentions.

Incompatibility

When couples ascribe negative motivations to their spouses, it often accompanies the complaint that they are just not compatible. Whenever a couple says this, we always agree, saying that every couple is incompatible. They are incompatible simply for the reason that one is male and the other is female. The differences between male and female are enough to make every marriage an incompatible relationship. Then you add on top of that our personality differences, our family background differences, and our differences in expectations and you wonder sometimes how any couple makes something good out of all those differences.

When we don't give grace to each other, especially in regard to our differences, we eventually make the differences even larger than they are by polarizing them. If there is a part of Jan that I don't accept, the more I don't accept that part of her, the more she tries to get me to accept that part of her, until we are at opposite ends of the scale on the issue. How different our experience is when I accept with loving grace that part of her that is different. My extending grace helps her to relax about that area of her personality, and the more she relaxes, the more I give grace until eventually there is no issue about that part of her in our relationship. We have developed compatibility where there had been incompatibility. When our differences are embraced by each other, we are experiencing grace and love that feeds into keeping our love alive for each other.

The Free Gift of Grace

Giving grace is never earned. I can't say, "I would give you more grace if only you would ..." Grace is a gift we give each other freely. One expression of our giving grace to our spouses is the ability to forgive when they have failed us in some way. Followers of Christ are encouraged by the apostle Paul to forgive "one another, just as God through Christ has forgiven you" (Ephesians 4:32). How did God forgive us? He did so freely without any expectation of us except that we accept his forgiveness. We can't earn his forgiveness. We can't buy his forgiveness. It is just like grace—it is his gift to us.

Think what can happen in a marriage when we can freely give grace and forgiveness to each other, especially when we can act and believe that our spouses' motives and intentions are for the best, even when it doesn't seem that way to us. That's what it means to give each other grace.

SUMMARY

We trust that your marriage has been enriched as you have journeyed this path toward greatness with us. Our prayer is that you will, in the words of the prophet Malachi, "Guard your heart; remain loyal to the wife of your youth" (Malachi 2:15).

Perhaps Archibald MacLeish had that passage in mind as he wrote "The Old Gray Couple."

She:	*Love, says the poet, has no reasons.*
He:	*Not even after fifty years?*
She:	*Particularly after fifty years.*
He:	*What was it, then, that lured us, that still teases?*
She:	*You used to say my plaited hair!*
He:	*And then you'd laugh.*
She:	*Because it wasn't plaited.*
	Love has no reason, so you made one up
	to laugh at. Look! The old, gray couple!
He:	*No, to prove the adage true:*
	Love has no reasons, but old lovers do.
She:	*And they can't tell.*

He: *I can and so can you.*
          Fifty years ago we drew each other,
          magnetized needle toward the longing north.
          It was your naked presence that so moved me.
          It was your absolute presence that was love.

She: *Ah, was!*

He: *And now, years older, we begin to see*
          absence not presence: what the world would be
          without your footstep in the world—the garden
          empty of the radiance where you are.

She: *And that's your reason?—that old lovers see*
          their love because they know now what its loss will be?

He: *Because like Cleopatra in the play,*
          they know there's nothing left once love's away . . .

She: *Nothing remarkable beneath the visiting moon . . .*

He: *Ours is the late, last wisdom of the afternoon.*
          We know that love, like light, grows dearer toward
          the dark.[4]

Every couple on their wedding day plans to become over the years that "old gray couple." May your love grow dearer with each passing day. I'm confident that it will as you remain committed to God and to each other, taking to heart and putting into practice the seven secrets of a successful marriage.

1 Jack O. and Judith K. Balswick, *A Model for Marriage* (Downers Grove, IL: IVP Academic, 2006), 40.

2 John M. Gottman, *Marital Therapy: A Research-Based Approach* (Seattle: The Gottman Institute, Inc., 2000–2001), 10.

3 Balswicks, *A Model for Marriage*, 49.

4 Archibald MacLeish, "The Old Gray Couple," *Collected Poems 1917 to 1982* (Boston, MA: Houghton Mifflin, 1985), 33.